What People A̸
Conscious Wome₁

CW01073118

These heart-warming stories wi
and absolute clarity, they shine a light on the issues we all wrestle
with. Told lovingly, with a disarming honesty, they ensure that you'll
learn, laugh and cry as you read this book. It needs to be on your
shelf. You'll turn to it again and again.

~ Cathleen Fillmore, President, Speakers Gold Bureau

In *Conscious Women, Conscious Careers*, Darlene Montgomery uses
the power of story to show God intervening in people's lives to
assist, heal, uplift, and guide them in extraordinary ways, even in the
smallest details. This book demonstrates that the journey of discovering your mission requires trust, courage, faith, patience, stillness,
and tuning into a higher power to learn what it is you were meant to
do and how to go about fulfilling your sacred contract with life.

~ Linda Anderson, inspirational speaker and author of
*Angel Dogs, Angel Cats, Angel Horses, God's Messengers:
What Animals Teach Us about the Divine*, and *35 Golden Keys to
Who You Are & Why You're Here*

As an intuitive, I meet and guide many women (and men) along their
path. Darlene has, with her books, taken it a step further. Making big
transitions in our lives is important, but it is much more rewarding
when we can write about them and share with others. Darlene's
books are gifts that keep giving!

~ Carole Matthews, Intuitive Medium, columnist,
and radio broadcaster

These inspirational stories offer hope and expanded perspective and reverberate with possibility. They reveal women creating and living their dreams and finding meaning and higher purpose in their work. They remind us that the universe shows up in mysterious and wondrous ways to support and guide us on our path and that it's as important to be grateful for each step of the unfolding process as it is to celebrate the result.

~ Alissa Lukara, author of *Riding Grace: A Triumph of the Soul*
(Silver Light Publications, scheduled pub. date February 2007)
and president of Lifechallenges.org, the Cybercenter for
Living Creatively with Life's Challenges.

A pure gift for bringing out the most vital aspects of a narrative … offering a clear, crisp, interpretation … like a magnet, attracting wonderful stories from all over the world. Yes, her name is Darlene Montgomery … and she is simply amazing.

~ Judee Regan, Author, *We Don't Die Well In The Western World:*
A Message of Hope and Meaningful Work …
the Entrepreneurial Way.

I could not get enough of the stories in *Conscious Women, Conscious Lives*. I looked forward to reading them at bedtime after painting all day. So when I came to the last story, I was craving for more. I feel like I am in *Conscious Women* withdrawal, so much so that I will read the book all over again … and again … until there is a Book 3. Well Done!!!!!!!

~ Susan Duplan, Artist

Conscious Women
Conscious Careers

Conscious Women
Conscious Careers

Life Changing Stories

Edited by
Darlene Montgomery

From the Social Issues Series:
White Knight's Remarkable Women

White Knight Books
Toronto, Canada

Published in 2006 by
White Knight Books, a division of Bill Belfontaine Ltd.
Suite 103, One Benvenuto Place, Toronto Ontario Canada M4V 2L1
T. 416-925-6458 F. 416-925-4165 • e-mail whitekn@istar.ca
www.whiteknightbooks.ca

White Knight Books gratefully acknowledges the financial support of the Ontario Media Development Corporation and the Ontario Arts Council.

Ordering information

CANADA	UNITED STATES
White Knight Books	APG Distributors
c/o Georgetown Terminal Warehouses	(Associated Publishers' Group)
34 Armstrong Avenue,	1501 County Hospital Road
Georgetown ON, L7G 4R9	Nashville, TN, 37218 USA
T: 1-866-485-5556 F: 1-866-485-6665	T: 1-888-725-2606 F: 1-800-510-3650

First printing: April 2006

Library and Archives Canada Cataloguing in Publication
Conscious women, conscious careers : book three / Darlene Montgomery, editor.
Sequel to: Conscious women, conscious lives, books 1 and 2.
ISBN 0-9736705-9-2
1. Self-help techniques. 2. Women. I. Montgomery, Darlene, 1958-
BF632.C653 2006   158.1   C2006-900363-7

Cover Art:
Cover and Text Design: Karen Thomas Petherick
Edited by Laura Reave
Back Cover Picture: Christine Switzer
Printed and Bound in Canada

Permissions:
"Introduction" from THE ARTIST'S WAY by Julia Cameron, copyright © 1992 by Julia Cameron. Used by permission of Jeremy P. Tarcher, an imprint of Penguin group (USA) Inc.

Dedication

This book is dedicated to women everywhere

Contents

Chapter Four:
THE GIFT OF HIGHER VISION

Chapter Five:
THE COURAGE TO BELIEVE

Acknowledgements

Conscious Careers has been a joy to compile. With each new story that came across my desk, I was more and more astounded to witness the spiritual insight and depth of experience of each writer. I am so grateful that I am able to be part of the process of creating these books, but the greatest reward comes in interacting with the many contributors from all walks of life. Thanks to each and every one of you who shared your story, your challenges, and your breakthroughs.

I often hear from readers who have gained so much spiritually, emotionally and mentally from that hidden ingredient in the stories in the *Conscious Women* books. I know that many of you faced your fears to write your stories and for that I thank you. It is only because of your willingness to delve deeper and deeper that the stories offer a medicine for the Soul.

Thanks to my many good and true friends on the path of ECK-ANKAR, Jane and Paul Pulkys, Lily Bedikian, Yolande Savoie, Jerry and Jo Leonard, Janet Matthews, Thomas Drayton, Janine Smith, Barbara Russo-Smith, Marlene Chapelle, Barbara Allport, and Carole Lidstone, who have shared those special moments of insight and clarity on the path. I thank you with all my heart. A special thanks to Karen Thomas Petherick for her cover designs and to Bill Belfontaine for his courage and fortitude in bringing these books to the world. Thanks to Laura Reave for her editing work.

Thank you to each and every one who became a participant in creating this book.

And finally, a special thanks to Sri Harold Klemp for both outer and inner support.

~ *Darlene Montgomery*

Introduction

There is one thing in this world, which you must
never forget to do.
Human beings come into this world to do particular work.
That work is their purpose, and each is specific
to the person.
If you forget everything else and not this,
there's nothing to worry about.
If you remember everything else and forget your true work,
then you will have done nothing in your life.
— Rumi

Once I was confused about my life work. I spent weeks, months, and years deliberating over what would make me happy and content. I tried a number of professions but came up against a wall of dissatisfaction over and over again. Somewhere along the way, my dreams revealed that I had a purpose in being here. It came in the form of a dream that needed solving, and I spent years trying to understand my place in this universe.

One day, I was asked to tell a story at a conference. I'd never been asked to tell a story before. How hard could it be? But before I was to step on stage, I had no idea what I was to say. Then a voice whispered, Tell this story. It was a story of survival, and returning home after a long journey, one where I'd left behind a part of me that had lived in fear and separation from God. When I left the stage, I knew my purpose. It was written on the faces of each audience member. Tears ran down their faces. A strange awe hung in the air. I'd never experienced anything like it before, and I knew that I had stumbled upon something important.

It took some time to create the correct circumstances that would allow me to put together the books you are reading now, *Conscious Women—Conscious Lives* and now *Conscious Women—Conscious Careers*. My hope is that you will catch a glimpse of your own destiny in the stories on these pages. We often overlook our greatest purpose because it may seem like a glove we've always worn or a talent we've always had.

As I've collected and compiled these stories, I've witnessed the kind of transformation once thought possible only in biblical stories or in the lives of saints. Yet many who walk the earth today have had a direct experience with God or the Holy Spirit. Some have had encounters in dreams, others have heard an angelic voice, and still others have seen the light of God in one of its many forms.

These stories are a testimony to the everyday miracles in our lives.

~ *Darlene Montgomery*

1

Getting To Our Purpose

"God, please use me," is the most powerful affirmation we can say for an abundant career. It is the miracle-worker's prayer. Everybody wants a great job. Accept that it's already been given you. The fact that you're alive means a function has been assigned to you: open your heart to everyone and everything. That way you're a vessel of God. Don't worry about what to say or what to do. He'll let you know.

From *A Return to Love* by Marianne Williamson

Energy Medicine

All happenings, great and small, are parables
whereby God speaks.
The art of life is to get the message.
— Malcolm Muggeridge

I was, my mother tells me, born smiling, and the first energy I can recall feeling is the energy that wells into a smile. When I smile, it doesn't actually feel like I'm smiling. It feels more like an energy is smiling me.

I was born with a heart murmur, contracted tuberculosis at age five, had terrible food allergies and hay fever, showed the first symptom of what was later diagnosed as multiple sclerosis when I was sixteen, had a mild heart attack by my late twenties, had sever asthma in my early thirties, and a breast tumor at thirty-four. In addition, I have struggled with severe PMS, and hypoglycemia since age twelve.

By my early thirties, my health was extremely precarious. I retreated to Fiji to live a very basic life. Early in my stay, I was bitten by a poisonous insect. Because my immune system was already badly impaired, I had no resistance to the bite. I became very sick and went in and out of a coma. It seemed I might die.

But the shamans of Vatukarasa, a nearby village, learning of my plight, came with a treatment for the bite. They buried me up to my neck in the sand and left me there for long stretches several times each day over a forty-eight-hour period. They believed the toxins would be drained into the sand. I recovered. This was one of the many incidents that turned the wheel, setting my course toward healing work.

My health returned while I was in Fiji. My family and I lived in the wild, far from the nearest town. We swam in the ocean every day. We ate breadfruit from the ground and fish from the sea. Nothing was processed. Nothing was canned. Everything was organic. There were no fumes from cars and no chemicals in our clothing. Life was lived at a slow pace. It was a world where you could just be. There was no radio, no newspaper, no television. After a time, I wasn't even sure the United States still existed.

When I returned to the States in 1977, I went into a culture shock. My taste buds had become so sharp that I felt assaulted by the chemicals in the foods I ate. I wanted to move to some tiny town, to get away from the cities and the pollution. I wanted to raise my daughters in a healthy world. But my marriage was ending, and I didn't know how I was going to make a living.

Even though healing work came naturally to me, I had no idea that feeling and seeing energies, a talent I'd had since childhood, could lead to a career. I had taken a pre-med curriculum in college, but my sensibilities were offended by an approach to health that was based more on what you could learn from cadavers than what you could learn from the body's living energies.

Shortly after returning to Fiji, through one of the more striking synchronicities in my life, I wound up in a Touch for Health instructor training course. I learned about this approach to healing after I encountered a woman wearing a T-shirt inscribed with a picture of a hand and the words, "Touch for Health." When I asked her about it, her reply was, "Oh, I'm so excited! I'm leaving next week to be trained as a Touch for Health instructor." I felt lightning strike. I still didn't know what Touch for Health was, but I heard myself say, "Me too."

She gave me a phone number. I called the Touch for Health Office to have them send me information. They made one of those serendipitous errors that changes a person's destiny and sent me a letter congratulating me for having successfully completed the basic Touch for Health classes, which were the prerequisites for attending the teachers' training. The next teachers' training began the following Tuesday. Off I went.

Everybody else there had a solid foundation in Touch for Health system. While I had never before been exposed to any training in alternative medical practices, I had the sense that I had come home to something that was deeply familiar. The training was ideal for me. Touch for Health gave me a structure that balanced my intuitive nature and a form with which to work with the energies I could already see and intuit. Its use of muscle testing—which I also call energy testing—gave me a tool to demonstrate for a client or a student what I was seeing.

One of the first classes I taught was at a retirement home. A man well into his eighties had been paralyzed on his right side by a stroke a few months earlier, and he was extremely depressed. He wondered why his life had to be dragged out, bemoaned the fact that he had survived the stroke, and wished he were dead. With no feeling or control on his right side, he couldn't do the physical exercises designed to improve the flow of his energy.

Reaching for a way to help him, I asked him to sit in front of a mirror and imagine seeing himself doing exercises that cross energy over from each brain hemisphere to the opposite side of the body. I encouraged him to "see" the energy radiating light, color, and power to the frozen side. He did this every day for several days. Feelings began to return to the paralyzed side of his body. He had been told he would never have feeling or movement there again. But by the time the class ended twelve weeks later, he had enough movement in his right arm and leg that he could perform rather than only imagine the exercises. He was so excited to see that his mind had reactivated his body that his whole self-concept shifted.

I tend to vibrate to the energies of other people. At times I feel like a tuning fork. I see and sense other people's energies as rhythms and vibrations, frequencies and flows, jolts and currents, colorful swirls and geometric patterns. Early in my life, I came to understand that the colors, shapes, movements, and textures I saw held meaning.

As a fourth grader, I once overheard a number of teachers gossiping about my teacher, Miss Proctor, belittling her intelligence, ridiculing her as strange and eccentric, and wondering out loud how she ever got through college. I was shocked and totally puzzled. Were they blind? The strongest thing about Miss Proctor was a beautiful, pale, creamy yellow energy emanating from her body that said volumes to me. Intuitively, I knew it meant she was both kind and wise. She led with a sort of innocence, but it seemed obvious to me that she was an advanced and trustworthy being. Her peers, as I later came to understand, would have found it easier to respect her had she assumed a sophisticated demeanor rather than being so spontaneous and carefree.

To this day, my appraisals of people are based on the subtle energies I feel and see emanating from them, not on their words, physical appearances, status, or personality. This quirk has proven invaluable in my work. I have learned over the years not only to understand that what I see and feel in a person's energies has meaning, but also to use my hands to weave these energies to improve a person's health, vitality, and clarity of mind. Matter follows. This is the fundamental law of energy medicine. When your energies are vibrant, so is your body.

~ *Donna Eden*

A Road Less Traveled

If you do not feel yourself growing in your work
and your life broadening and deepening,
if your task is not a perpetual tonic to you,
you have not found your place.
— Orison Swett Marden (1850-1924)
Founder of Success Magazine

It was a beautiful, sunny July day, but I was reluctant to go outside for some long overdue exercise in the middle of my workday. I was grudgingly convinced, though, after a phone call from my concerned mother, who had tried for many weeks to get me to go out for a nice walk in the sunshine. I gave in, sullen at first, but with a warmth growing within that soon matched the weather.

As I walked, I thought of my life, of the choices I was too afraid to make, caught reluctantly in a world of money shifters and financial planners. For the first time in my life I was making really good money, and the din and clatter drove out the truth for a while. I'd recently bought a house, and the noise of this long-awaited moment of accomplishment for me, a single mother, was music to my ears, so I chose not to listen to the tiny, frail voice inside that kept saying, "You know what you've got to do. Why are you stalling with these distractions? Don't be afraid to go." But afraid I was.

I had been struggling with my lifelong desire to be an entrepreneur because none of my businesses ever really brought in enough money to sustain my family. Maybe this job was where I should remain and dedicate my energies. After all, I thought, I'm getting raises and recognition from my boss and co-workers in a way I never had before. Convincing and beguiling was this chatter.

Swirling around in my head like litter on a windy day came the other uninvited guests to this noisy party. As I thought of the decision I'd made to file for personal bankruptcy a few years ago and how much of a failure I felt until I'd taken this job, down came my mood. I thought then of a more recent choice, motivated by all the other financial planners that surrounded me at work, to sign up for and begin studying for my Certified Financial Planner designation. Up swung my mood. It was easy to see why I was so convinced that this was my path, until my path was interrupted during my walk by a fork in the road—literally. I can still remember standing there for what seemed like an eternity. In reality it was probably more like seconds that I looked at one route and then the other trying to decide in my few remaining minutes of lunch break left, which road to choose. A look to the right revealed some city workers working on the road. I grimaced, anticipating the attention that a woman in a skirt and tank top (I had removed my suit jacket to take in the sunshine) would produce. Then I looked left to the inhabitant-free road that beckoned. I went left.

Within seconds of my decision, I lay sprawled face down on the asphalt, with a concussion, a front tooth missing, a displaced hip, and more bruises and scrapes than I cared to count. Ironically, in attempting to avoid the construction workers, I had just been hit by one driving a pickup truck. My life would never be the same again.

I took four months off to convalesce. During those months when I could barely move, I thought of my life direction again, but this time the fork I approached was in my mind. In those four months I tried very hard to study, but something was different. I came to the realization that my purpose in life was to teach, to write, and to guide others as well as myself.

I gave up my ready-made career as a financial planner, with the potential to make a lot of money, for a life of my own design, even if that choice required some ups and downs to get there. I learned to live with the extremely uncomfortable feeling of not knowing what the devil that new life would look like. I began studying for my coaching certificate, but most of all, I finally started listening. I listened to the little voice that had told me time and again to send out the manuscript that I had written three years prior that was just sitting in a drawer collecting dust.

Within three months of sending it out to the first publisher, I got a contract, and four months later I received my very first book advance. Both of these events are highly unusual for a first-time writer, but they happened to me, and I believe they happened because I listened. I realized then that life can run a lot more smoothly if we pay attention and have the courage to take in hand our Greater Purpose.

Now that my book is published and in stores, appearances in front of the media have become more of a regular occurrence. I see why I chose to avoid the original route that eventful day. On some level I knew that following through with my Greater Purpose—writing, teaching, guiding—would entail a lot of attention, attention I was not yet ready to receive. But once a commitment to an agreement is made, there is no turning back, and the work must be done. Make no mistake, though, I am thrilled at finding success and fulfillment with my writing and coaching, at finally finding my unique contribution to humanity!

Often I think of the many different ways I tried to find out what I was put here to do. My relentless questioning led me through so many jobs and start-ups in so many countries in my short 38 years that I always found it hard to accept that my life looked so vastly different than, say, a corporate executive or someone who found success with a first business. I envied people like that before the accident, before realizing that in order to be a good coach it's so important to be able to understand where others are coming from on a deep level. My understanding was earned by all the trials my life has taken me through. I have always felt compelled to take the road less traveled, and as Robert Frost says in his poem "The Road Not Taken," "…that has made all the difference."

~ *Maxine Hyndman*

Spreading My Wings

Each of us has an inner dream that we can unfold if we will
just have the courage to admit what it is. And the faith to
trust our own admission. The admitting is often very difficult.
— Julia Cameron

I sold my house. I sold some art and jewelry. And downsized my car. I knew that my choice meant a totally different standard of living, one that I hadn't experienced since my early 20s. My daughter cautioned, "I know you want to spread your wings, Mom, but don't lose too many feathers."

But I knew I had no choice. I knew that I couldn't lie to myself anymore. So I started to search.

Six months previously, on the flight home from Colorado, I pondered the advice given to me by an industrial psychologist. "Just place the report on his desk and leave. That way he won't have to see you when he reads the report."

The "He" was my international boss, who was so intimidated by me that he would turn away from me behind his desk when I entered his office. In fact, I often had a secret game I played during some of our corporate cocktail get-togethers after regional meetings, when I would be standing drink in hand chatting with … let's call him James. He would back away from me; I'd take two steps forward. He'd back two steps, I'd back two steps, and he would come forward two steps. He didn't even know he was dancing! But it was the only fun in a very tedious, diminishing, but exhilarating time in my career. The report was the result of a week of scrutiny by myself and 11 other international CEOs who participated in a program called "Leadership at the Peak."

We had been monitored by six industrial psychologists so that we could know our weaknesses and celebrate our strengths. I had been voted the second leader of the group, and my score for creativity and entrepreneurship was off the scale: "Highly valuable skills and instincts." I had also made some lasting friendships. But most importantly, I was now aware that my success wasn't luck. I was intelligent, intuitive, and hard working, and I deserved my success.

Just that alone was like receiving a box of gold. I wouldn't have to try so hard. I wouldn't have to run just to stand still. And most importantly, I wouldn't have to put up with the nonsense I received as one of the very few senior women in this worldwide company.

It was time to make a decision. Not just about how to present the results, but about how to live my life. Because, in truth, I was so very tired of 'handling' my boss and his boss. I was tired of the politics, tired of the game playing, and tired of pretending that I enjoyed it all.

The saying, "Be careful what you wish for because you may get it" came true. A few months later, the company made me an offer I couldn't refuse—they were closing down in Canada, and I received a fabulous golden handshake that would allow me to take as much time as I needed to think about myself and my future.

Headhunters called with VERY lucrative offers, and one in particular was really intriguing: a start-up proposition for Canada with shares on the ground floor. Part of me wanted to accept, and part of me felt that would mean selling out again. So I went on a two-week mountain trek and lost myself in the midst of the extraordinary grandeur of the Canadian Rockies. By the second week, I knew there was no going back.

But forward to … where?

The search. I took classes: Reiki, Color Therapy, Meditation, EFT, Psycho-drama, short story writing, yoga, Spanish. I played with the idea of becoming a real estate agent, a massage therapist, a corporate facilitator, an Avon rep, and a cat breeder and boarder ("Oh perleeease!" said same daughter). I studied Kabbalah, First Nations folklore, White Magic, Buddhism, gardening, and Feng Shui. I became a Rosicrucian member. Nothing grabbed. Nothing took hold.

I read a lot. Watched the squirrels in the garden free-dive onto the bird feeder from the overhead wires. Entertained. Cooked and baked. Hiked. Wrote a few speeches for clients. And did a lot of nothing.

For a while, it was wonderful. But I was beginning to get itchy. I knew I had a passion out there … somewhere.

Then one day I saw an ad for a basic hypnosis class. I signed up. The instructor was uninspiring, but the material was powerful and profound. I knew this was IT.

I did a quick survey of the marketplace and potential and realized how little money I would be bringing in for the foreseeable future. That's when I started selling. The house. The art. The jewelry. And it didn't seem to matter. I was learning more and more about hypnosis and the magic it can create.

With my background, starting a school was a natural idea, teaching people how to work with themselves and others to access their powerful subconscious mind. I developed the positioning for the clinic and school: "A warm and welcoming place to learn and grow." Now, eight years later, we are thriving, with classes most weekends and a clinic which bustles seven days a week helping students and clients to find their own magnificence. I am now teaching hypnosis and past life regression around the world. I have published a book about it, and I regularly appear on the Shirley MacLaine website to host the chat room discussing hypnosis. This is a very different life from that of ten years ago.

What do I miss? Not much. Occasionally, in the depth of winter, I miss the resources to take off for a long weekend in the warm sunshine, or a rejuvenating trip to a spa. But that's about it.

The work is magical. I am honored, humbled, and very grateful to be invited into people's lives so that I can show them how to find their light and magnificence.

And I wouldn't change it for the world.

~ Dr. Georgina Cannon

It's Personal

Everything is personal, every blessed thing.
The sunset. The sunrise. The robin's song in spring.
Everything is personal, as I wend my weary way
Through a lonely nighttime vigil, into the break of day.

Everything is personal, sent from God above;
His grace, and all His blessings, especially His love.
He finds me irresistible. I can't imagine why;
For me, He sends the rainbow to paint the azure sky.

For me, He dots the darkened sky, with tiny, twinkling light.
For me, He sets my soul on fire, long into the night.
To Him I turn my weary soul, when all my hopes are gone,
Then once again He proves to me, He's loved me all along.

I can't explain this personal friendship that I feel.
I only know within my heart that He is very real.
Trees and flowers, birds and bees are personal, you see;
Because I'm certain that my God created them for me!

~ *Jaye Lewis*

How Césan Got Her Groove Back

Art may not change anything ... but the ideas we have about
ourselves we project into the world ... Negative images have a
way of coming alive just as positive images have. If we project
images of beauty, hope, healing, courage, survival, co-oper-
ation, interrelatedness, serenity, imagination and harmony,
this will have a positive effect. Imagine what artists could do
if they became committed to the long-term good of the
planet. The possibilities are beyond imagination. If all artists
would ever pull together for the survival of humankind, it
would be a power such as the world has never known.

— Ciel Bergman

There is a film called "How Stella Got Her Groove Back." If this story
had a humorous title, it could probably be called "How Césan Got
Her Groove Back." Another possible, more serious title could be "The
Battle for Césan's Soul." In truth, it's the battle for the soul that helps
you get your groove back. At least, this is what I've learned.

Three years ago I was in yet another of a long series of careers
that didn't quite fit.

Struggling, unhappy with myself, fearful, secretly depressed. By
any standards I had an excellent job: an adequate, reliable income
with full health benefits for my whole family, a location close to home,
a progressive work environment, a noble profession ... Nevertheless,

I was going crazy because I thought I should be content with this and I wasn't. I was going crazy because I knew I just wasn't in my groove, not groovy, not grooving at all.

I felt all this energy pent up in me, wadded and stuck and pushing to get out. It seemed like I'd been in this state for years, and I really didn't think I'd last much longer unless I did something about it. Finally, the fear of what I might find became insignificant compared to the fear of what would happen if I continued to ignore it.

Once you're willing to accept the truth, it's usually pretty easy to see. In my case I had known for years, at least 15, that I wanted to be an artist. It was not that I had been to art school. I hadn't. I had done some creative work here and there along the way, and there was simply a feeling, a dawning revelation that I came here to create.

I believed that to deny this calling would have been to slowly fall apart from the inside. I had no choice, really—I had to go forward with it.

> *Do what you love, and the money will follow.*
> *Be bold, and unseen forces will come to your aid.*
> *Build it, and they will come.*
> *To thine own self be true.*
> *Damn the torpedoes!*

I was determined to be an artist and sell my art. I knew I had the creative juice. And as for the business part, well, I'd post-produced a feature film, I'd managed a thriving therapy clinic, I'd led corporate workshops, I'd taught adolescents, I was a mother, for heaven's sake. I guessed I could figure the business part out. I'd have to, anyway, because I wasn't about to let it stop me.

There is a story of a commander of a squadron of ships who landed on a beach with his troops only to find that they were vastly outnumbered by the enemy. But they won the battle. Why? Because the first order the commander made was for his troops to burn their own ships. It is a brilliant strategy, really. No retreat was possible. He had left his troops no choice but to win or die trying. This is pretty much how I felt about my decision. I resolved not to back down.

I've heard that the most difficult part of getting what we want, actually, is to know what we want. I felt totally clear, and really, surely, that was half the battle. With my firm resolve and the support of my husband Mark …

I handed in my notice at my job, finished up my contract, transformed my home office into studio space, invested in art supplies, and started to do some painting. I was doing what I loved … I was being bold … and I waited for the unseen forces.

Now don't get me wrong, I do truly believe that the unseen forces do come to our aid. It must be said, however, that unseen forces have a style and schedule all their own.

Just because we have a Revelation, just because it is exactly what our Destiny might be, we don't always herald the triumphant victory that we might expect or hope for.

A Revelation (and the more powerful it is, the truer this is) is actually more like a battle cry. Fear, being the keeper of the personality's status quo, senses a change, an aspiration to a higher level of being, and basically goes nuts. As we will ourselves to higher purposes and take the revelatory faith-based leap, fear sounds the alarm on behalf of the old personality. Thus begins the battle for the soul. The enemy is merciless.

When I left my job, our family income decreased to the point that we had to remove our daughters from the private school that had been their beloved home and community for eight wonderful years. We sorely missed our extended healthcare benefits. Debts that we had started to pay off started to build up again with alarming speed.

Family and friends had a whole continuum of judgments and criticisms and concerns. One family member who had been to art school said that a teacher whom she greatly admired told her that if you're going to be an artist, better be a plumber too. This, she said, was the best advice she'd ever received. Another friend said, "Oh yeah, do what you love and to hell with the money, right?!" Even my closest friends would say sympathetically, "What a hard way to earn a living." Other artists would complain about how difficult it is to get your work out. How difficult to show it, how difficult to sell it. My mom was concerned I would expect too much. She was worried I had set my sights too high.

The art supplies were expensive, as I was using highest quality paints and products available. The credit card debt was building … and I wasn't even doing that much painting. Things kept coming up, preventing me from getting into the studio, plus I had discovered just how intimidating blank canvases can be. The work I did manage to complete didn't look all that great, I thought, and then someone suggested maybe I should go to art school …

I was pretty certain I was the worst wife and mother in the world, financially irresponsible, idealistic, a dreamer, impractical and naïve. And, just maybe, I was wrong about my artistic ability. I started to scan the jobs section of the paper instead of painting, to do the laundry instead of painting, to worry instead of painting…

And then a couple of months after I had started on my new path, I began to have some health problems. Over the next four months, my health became progressively worse. Numbness in my hands and feet, shooting pain up my arms and legs, exhaustion, dizziness, nausea, mental confusion—I was a basket case, and my family was terribly worried.

My glorious decision, my Great Calling was fading like a mirage. I thought I might be dying or worse.

I felt completely defeated. Here was the proof that the enemy, fear, was looking for: the proof that would keep me cowering on my knees forever. I simply didn't have the right stuff to be a successful artist. It was clear that I should give up—the fears and insecurities were overwhelming at this point.

Looking back on that time, three years ago, I'm just now beginning to recognize the significance of it. My healing crisis, my dark night of the soul, my ultimate test … just how resolved was I?

In a dark and tightly bound cocoon space, with all our energy drawn inwards, we give birth to incredible new aspects of ourselves. In my case, I now know that I was forging the tool belt of skills I would need to manifest my dream.

I collapsed because I needed to pause. I needed to gather my forces. I would need many to go where I was intending to go.

The subconscious negativities I carried about being an artist, about getting what I wanted, about following my bliss, had caught up with me and taken over. I was possessed by my own crap—a curse? Well, in the end, a blessing.

When it finally became clear that the doctors and tests couldn't find anything wrong, and it was clear that whatever it was, was not life-threatening and that I was not in fact deteriorating from some terrible disease, I gradually accepted that it was up to me to find a way out for myself. And here's the blessing. The pause, the collapse, the dis-ease, forced me to examine everything. To look at what was working and serving me and, oh boy, to look at what wasn't working and wasn't serving me.

Well, that part of the journey is a whole other story—suffice it to say that I cleared and cleansed and cleared and cleansed, and I'm still clearing and cleansing.

What we fear we draw towards us. It's how we pray for what we don't want. Very effective, from my experience. Even though I was clear enough to see my Destiny path, I was avoiding the self-examination of all my fears and doubts about being able to paint for a living. And so what happened? The fears and doubts kept manifesting as obstacles on my path: financial problems, negative judgments from others, diversions of all sorts, and finally illness.

At last, when I was unable even to move off my couch and pick up a paintbrush, I was forced to wake up. I was forced to bring the rest of my self to a new level, the level of the successful artist I so wished to become.

I was forced to seriously commit to my personal development. I mean real commitment—a daily, hourly, constant commitment to becoming more aware and more awake. What I learned was that the battles are not won any other way.

As we awaken to our greatest fears, the obstacles in the outside world begin to dissolve … such a powerful lesson to come my way.

The battle for César's soul is surely going to continue for some time. But I will not retreat. I burned my ships. Remember what an effective strategy that was?

Two and a half years ago, one year after making my Resolution to paint and six months after I became ill, I sold a painting for $180. The rest of that year I sold enough to cover all my start-up costs and expenses plus a bit extra. The next year I more than quadrupled my income from the previous year and was fetching up to $2800 for a painting. This year I've had work in the windows of two major galleries in Toronto, had paintings shipped to the US and Europe, sold rights for four of my paintings to be used on a postcard series, and was hired to do a number of commissioned paintings.

My daughters have grown a lot from their experiences in their new school and from seeing their mother succeed, my family and friends have given up their negativities, and I dare say they are even inspired. The relative whose teacher suggested being a plumber to support an art career? She is now one of my biggest supporters and has herself sold many of my paintings. The friend who said do what you love and to hell with the money? He has asked me when he can come over for some advice about selling his artwork. Most of the time the pile of laundry does not take priority over my painting, and I hardly ever look at the jobs section in the paper anymore. Anyway, I'm too busy with my new career, the one where I Got My Groove Back.

~ *César d'Ornellas Levine*

Becoming Who I Really Am

Energy is the essence of life. Every day you decide how you're going to use it by knowing what you want and what it takes to reach that goal, and by maintaining focus.
— Oprah Winfrey

It was the summer of 2004 and from a hospital bed late at night, I took stock of my life. It seemed I was moving toward the worst possible end to a journey that had begun back in 1998 when a spiritual question first imposed itself on me. The question had plagued me for years now, often showing up in tarot spreads, in psychic readings, and in angel card messages, asking, "Why are you not being who you really are?"

Maybe I was going to run out of time before it was fully answered.

The doctors who admitted me after a long day of treatment and tests in the emergency room thought I had a cancerous brain tumor and were concerned that it might be in a difficult place to access surgically. An MRI had been ordered, and specialists would review everything within the next few days.

Cold and alone, head throbbing, I forced myself to calm down. I thought, "God wouldn't take me now, when I am so close to finding my answer."

Whenever the question appeared, an overwhelming feeling of failure came with it. As a career banker in a senior position with a good income, I was happy with my life. The job had even improved over the years because, as a coach, I was helping people discover and reach their potential, so I felt I was fulfilling my goal of serving others through my work. But this feeling that I was to do something more with my life and time simply wouldn't let up.

Then in the spring of 2002, some friends and I met with a clairvoyant. When it came my turn to receive a short reading, she cocked her head to the side as if to listen to a message from some distant place. Nodding, she gently asked me, "Why are you not being who you really are?" Exasperated, I tried to get her to say more. She explained it was not for her to reveal, but her advice was, "Let go of the fear that is keeping you from your real purpose."

For several weeks afterward, I visualized my soul opening while asking, "Please help me understand my real purpose." Then I forgot all about it—until the breakthrough came.

That August, nearing home on the final leg of a road trip to Eastern Canada, I finally received "The Big Answer." Three of my closest friends and I were taking a break in a shady spot off the highway, reliving our week of adventure. After a few minutes I felt a tingling in my body, and everything fell silent. An energy rose from my solar plexus, breaking through blockages as it moved painfully toward my throat. To my surprise and the surprise of everyone else, my mouth opened and these words came out: "I'm going to write a book about what happened to us on our trip." Then dramatically, the long-awaited answer burst through. "I am a writer." These simple words left me with a calm feeling of relief.

But although I'd had a profound realization, I didn't know how to get started. What had seemed so obvious in the car was obviously not the whole answer, because over the next two years I didn't write a thing. I just worried and wondered, "Do I quit my job as a banker to be a writer?"

Back at square one, the relief was replaced by a kind of everything's-all-wrong anguish. At the start of my 2004 summer vacation I found I was completely miserable. My head had begun to ache every day. I knew I wasn't just physically sick: I was spiritually sick. Clearly, I needed help.

As the second week of my holidays wound down, something compelled me to leave the safety of my house where I'd been bedridden and head to our local bookstore. I felt drawn to the self-help section by some magic force. As my hand reached for a paperback entitled *Conscious Women—Conscious Lives: Powerful Stories of Healing Body, Mind, and Soul,* an electric sensation passed from my fingertips through my wrist and up my arm. As I held it, I knew the book contained important messages for me.

That afternoon, reading its stories on a park bench by Lake Ontario, I experienced an intense revelation as I felt a healing release of laughter and tears wash over me. Many of the storytellers in the book were describing how they had triumphed over struggles much like mine, trying to find answers as to who they are and why they are here.

One story in particular jumped out. It was of a radio host dealing with the fear and remorse she experienced when she was fired from her job of fourteen years and how she had found so much meaning in her difficulties. While I read it, tears flowed down my cheeks as I began to grasp a more complete answer to the question that had plagued me for so long. What I'd been missing was in the book, in the content of each story. Each one dealt with healing and awareness of life purpose.

I received a powerful confirmation of this at 6:00 the next morning when I turned on the television to see the face of an attractive woman conducting an interview. I was amazed to learn it was the very same woman whose story I'd read the evening before!

That afternoon, though, found me in the emergency room waiting area, seated on a plastic chair with my eyes closed. It was taking all my concentration to manage the blinding pressure of the migraine in the noisy, crowded room. Above the din, a snippet of conversation struck me. "I have no reason to be afraid," said a lady to her companion. In a heartbeat I heard a loud click inside my head. It sounded like a door unlocking—then I felt an idea push the door open. My need to record the idea was so great I forgot the pressure behind my eyes and dug for the note pad in my purse. Opening it, I began to write a story.

Soon after, a nurse called out my name, then ushered me into an examining room. With the young resident's words, "The CAT scan is showing a mass in your brain," all thought of the story disappeared.

It took almost a week to finally rule out the brain tumor and to confirm that what the doctors were seeing in the tests was evidence of a very old stroke that must have happened when I was a child. The neurological team worked for three more days to break the migraine episode. Back at home, I remained on leave while my prescribed medication was adjusted.

One seemingly ordinary morning during that period, I approached my computer and finished the story I'd started that day in the ER waiting room. It told of a healing experience surrounding the deaths of both my parents. On impulse, I emailed the author of *Conscious Women—Conscious Lives*, a woman named Darlene Montgomery. I wanted to thank her for her book and the stories that had first comforted and then inspired me to pick up the pen. Proud of my accomplishment, I sent her what I had written, not knowing she was working on her latest project, *Conscious Women—Conscious Lives, Book Two.* Her reply came back quickly; she wanted to include my story in her new book. Though I could hardly believe what was happening, I was sure this outcome and even the headache were both part of discovering the plan God and I had created for me.

My brain episode was the wake-up call I needed to help me accept the messages life had been giving me all along. When I found *Conscious Women* that day in the bookstore, it was like holding up a

mirror that allowed me to remember my soul contract. That co
involves plumbing the depths of my own experiences, not only t
myself, but as a writer of stories that heal and connect others to their
own divine nature. I'm no longer plagued by the question, "Why are
you not being who you really are?" I have a gift to share, and it is so
much of who I am that I know I will never forget again.

~ Judy Prang

A Gift of Love

If you would have love, you must first give love.
And if you give divine love to others,
you shall have divine love for yourself.
— Harold Klemp, *Love the Keystone of Life*

Traveling on a train driven by a steam engine can seem both terrifying and exhilarating to a small four-year-old child. This was my very first travel experience in 1945, when my family moved from my birthplace in Lower Largo, Fife, to the lovely village of Ballachulish in Argyll, Scotland. The mountains there are as high as the lochs are deep, and the warm-hearted natives strive to live in harmony with their surroundings.

Because my dad was a minister, our new home was the United Free Church Manse, which had recently been built in front of the old church. There was no electricity in that area of Scotland at that time, so we burned peat or coal in the fireplace for heat and used paraffin lamps for light.

Behind the house and church flowed the Larach River, singing its way over large rocks and stones. Its daily song was an invitation to adventure and the mystery of what might be found on the other side. One day curiosity overcame me and, without thinking, I went against my dad's wishes and crossed the river. The only thing I remember about the other side is the distant image of my dad riding his bike home. In my hurry to jump from rock to rock before my dad saw me, I fell into the fast-moving current. Fortunately, my mom saw me from the kitchen window and hurried to pull me out of the icy water before my dad got home.

While sitting on our front lawn picking buttercups or making daisy chains, I would often drink in the beauty of the mountainside and gaze longingly at the local school which was situated across the road, behind the principal's house. It seemed to me that every child in the area went to school except my younger brother and me. Somehow, my fifth birthday seemed like an eternity away!

My patience wore away as this longing for knowledge grew, until one day I found myself banging my fists on the door of Miss Cameron's classroom, insisting that I be allowed to join the school. I had to persist in this fashion for several days before Miss Cameron finally relented and allowed me to enter her sacred domain. Within a few weeks, however, my joy quickly turned to sorrow as the whole class became ill with scarlet fever! Since it was an acute, febrile, contagious disease, there was a sudden mass exodus of children to the fever hospital a few miles from the village.

One night, in the middle of the night, my temperature spiked at 105 degrees Fahrenheit, and I had to be transported by taxi to the country hospital. In addition to a red rash, the pain in my nose, throat, and mouth was so severe that I was afraid to cry for fear of making my condition even more unbearable. Surely I must be dying! To make matters worse, I was also diagnosed with rheumatic fever. No visitors were allowed and so, once a week, my dad would ride into the hospital grounds on his bicycle, and I was allowed to wave to him from the window near my bed. He brought me gifts of "blood oranges" for my health, and those were shared with all the other children. Although the nurses were extremely busy, they were always very kind and compassionate.

Because of the rheumatic fever, I remained in hospital a lot longer than my classmates, and I was given a considerable amount of tender loving care by the staff. As a result of this experience, I knew at this tender young age that someday I would definitely become a nurse.

In 1959 I was accepted by The Western Infirmary in Glasgow for nurse's training and eventually became a registered nurse. I then moved to my parents' home in Paisley for a while so that I could train as a midwife. When I immigrated to Canada in 1967, I worked as a delivery room nurse because midwifery had not been legalized in this country at that time. I cared for many wonderful patients over the years, but there is one patient who will always stand out from the rest because her gratitude, under very painful circumstances, touched the very core of my heart. To protect her identity, I will call her Jean.

I was working in the delivery room assessment room one day when Jean, accompanied by her mom, arrived to be assessed. I learned that Jean's baby was overdue and that she hadn't felt any baby movements at all that day. Because the baby's father was no longer in the picture, Jean's mom had accompanied her for support. When the fetal monitor failed to pick up the baby's heartbeat, her doctor was notified and an ultrasound ordered. The dreaded answer came when the ultrasound confirmed that the baby had indeed died.

My heart went out in sympathy to this young mother and grandmother. I encouraged them to talk about their pain and feelings of loss, and I listened to them with an open heart. Eventually it was decided that Jean would go home for the night and come back for induction of labor the next morning.

When I came into work early the next day, I asked specifically if I could be assigned to Jean instead of working in the assessment room. Jean was pleased with this arrangement because of the bond of friendship that now existed between us. The induction of labor progressed well, and Jean was given an epidural so that her delivery would be a pain-free experience. When the delivery was imminent, her doctor was called in to deliver the baby. Jean delivered a beautiful, black-haired, stillborn baby girl.

When we saw the cord wrapped tightly around the baby's neck, we knew the reason for the baby's demise. I quickly washed the baby's face while the placenta was being delivered, and wrapped her up in a pink blanket for her mom and grandmother to hold. This was truly a most heartbreaking experience!

Deeply saddened, I cut a lock of dark hair for Jean to keep as a memento, along with a set of her baby's footprints. Jean wept as she held her baby for a long, long time before being transferred to a private room on the ward.

When I said goodbye to Jean that evening, I never dreamed that I would ever see her again. Two weeks later the delivery room doorbell rang, and over the intercom a woman asked to speak specifically to me. I opened the door, and to my great surprise Jean was standing there with a gift in her hand. Inside the box was a lovely Noritake fine china cup and saucer she had bought me to thank me for all my care. Along with the cup was a copy of the beautiful poem she had composed for her daughter.

This was probably one of the most touching moments of my life, as I thought of all the hundreds of mothers I had cared for who simply took their baby's life and health for granted. Despite her grief and pain, this lovely lady took the time to show me her gratitude. I had a hard time choking back the tears as I hugged her in thanks.

I have been retired from nursing for almost five years now. And on occasion, very early in the morning, you will find me sipping tea from a Noritake cup, thinking fond thoughts of Jean. I am pleased to say that many years later Jean, now happily married, delivered a healthy baby girl.

~ *Sybil Barbour*

A Soul Calling

You can have anything you want if you are willing
to give up the belief that you can't have it.
— Robert Anthony

At fifty-eight I decided to take a break. I had worked thirty-five years
without one, raising children and businesses, developing a career,
becoming addicted to eighty-hour work weeks. Don't get me wrong.
I loved my work. I traveled the Pacific, brokering private islands and
boutique resorts, working with clients from around the globe, mas-
tering complicated transactions in various jurisdictions. I took care
of my deals, my clients, my reps, and my children, but I probably
failed a good deal of the time to take care of myself. Some people hear
the whispers and learn from others' mistakes. Being a bit deaf to intuitive things, I had to make my own mistakes. I had to hear the screams.

The year 2001 shook me up. I had relocated to a very small island
in a new country to care for a dying friend (my Cook Islands affiliate),
his company, and his 13-year-old son, Daniel. I was directing and
managing an international corporation, and, just for kicks, remodel-
ing a 120-year-old house. To say it had not been an easy year would
be a gross understatement. I was exhausted physically, mentally, and
emotionally. Within a week after Peter died, I had performed the
service, scattered his ashes, hosted friends from afar who flew in for

the funeral, and found a home for Daniel with relatives in New Zealand. Finally, I found time to shed my own tears.

Then it began. Aches and pains started in the backs of my thighs, moving relentlessly into my back, shoulders, and neck. One day my arms went numb. I went to one doctor and then another. They tested and questioned, but found nothing. Yet the pain continued. I was on codeine by now, and it wasn't working. I went to the hospital. Surely the other doctors had missed something: a pinched nerve, a rare tropical disease. One by one, each possibility was eliminated.

I left the small clinic to join friends for lunch. It was our regular Friday at Trader Jack's, where the girls caught up with island snippets and watched the sun glisten on the ever-changing lagoon. Arriving first, I ordered a glass of wine to kick-start the pain pills. Then Laurie arrived, introducing herself. I had not met her before, but stood to greet her, and as we touched and embraced in the traditional manner, offering both cheeks, she stiffened, standing back startled.

"I'm so sorry," she exclaimed. She asked how long I had been in pain and what I was doing just before it began. How could she know? I had not mentioned it. "Your pain pills won't work," she went on. "It's not about your body. Your soul is calling you." Just then Mattie arrived. She told us that she had said nothing to Laurie, but that Laurie operated on a different wavelength than the rest of us. We settled in to enjoy the fresh catch, wine and conversation, and by two o'clock we embraced, signing off with "Let's do it again soon," and "Kiss, kiss". Then Laurie looked at me deeply. "Come by anytime," she invited.

Later that afternoon, racked with pain, and frightened now that none of the island doctors had a clue, I pulled my car onto the small island road and drove east to Muri Beach, per Laurie's directions. She did not have a telephone, so calling her first was out of the question. As was not going.

"I was expecting you," she said, inviting me in. She asked me to lie on the floor while she proceeded to place her hands just above my body, chanting something quietly. Falling into a deep calm, I noticed that the pain stopped, and it did not return.

When I got up, Laurie again looked into my depths. I stood, free of pain for the first time in weeks. It was simply gone. "You have to stop," she insisted. I wondered for a moment what, exactly, she had done, but I felt so good it never occurred to me to ask. I pondered her words. Then we discussed them. According to this healer, my pain was coming from my soul, telling me to stop. To stop working, stop working out, stop doing for others, stop running around ... to just stop. Then I could get quiet enough to listen to the whispers. I would miss the path if I did not take care to listen.

Laurie said she had another appointment, so I left, driving home as a mango-hued sunset splashed across the lagoon. How wonderful to be without pain! For the next few days I slowed down and gave serious thought to what Laurie had said. I noticed that whenever I sat at my computer, the pain returned, leaving the moment I got up, walked away, or crossed the road to watch daybreak or take a swim. But how could I stop? I needed to work, to earn. I couldn't even imagine stopping, shutting down. But I believed her directive, and little by little I opened to the possibility. Within three weeks, three pain-free weeks, I had notified my Hawaii office, my affiliates in Fiji and Tahiti, Vanuatu and Samoa, New Zealand, and Australia. I shut down my company websites, then e-mailed family and friends and all of our client mailing lists, doing everything I could think of to pre-pare for a one-year sabbatical. I even got excited, just thinking about it. Imagine me, taking a year off!

Just imagine. I would travel and garden and write. Yes! I would finish novels, collect my poems and short stories, and assemble a body of work that stretched back forty years. I would also spend long, languid afternoons lying in my hammock (still in a sealed bag, twenty years after I bought it) and floating in the lagoon. I would take a trip to Europe and another to Australia, visiting places and friends

I had never had the time to visit. And sure enough, by year's e.
shutdown went off without a hitch. The play part took center stage
I headed north to Hawaii for Christmas with my children and grandchildren. By early February I was celebrating my birthday with
friends on a private motu in Tahiti, lying topless in the shallows with
the girls, while a large Tahitian served us chilled French champagne,
baguettes, paté. I would remember this special day a week later as I
lay in post-op, looking down at my brown toes.

I had awakened the night before. I usually slept well, but I
couldn't sleep. I tossed and turned, finally getting up to boot up my
computer and finish some of the bookings for my upcoming European
trip. Then it happened. A stranger who had broken into my bathroom appeared suddenly, wearing my underwear, smashing a glass
into my face.

It did not occur to me to think. Some animal possessed my body
and took over all of the functions and processes I usually reason
through. As I fled, I didn't think about whether or not the attacker
was following or whether I was OK. I didn't wonder if I would get
away or if I would live or heal. Or if I would ever again see the
Cheshire moon rising through the needles of the ironwood trees that
danced on the lagoon's edge. I simply fled. Adrenaline kicked in, and
by the grace of God I got away and to a neighbor's. They stopped the
bleeding, called the ambulance, and stayed with me during the surgery and through the many uneasy dawns that followed.

Months of trauma, laced with high doses of high anxiety and
classic post-traumatic stress disorder symptoms such as hiding out,
hyper vigilance, convulsions and panic attacks—this was how I spent
my days and nights. The severe symptoms lessened with therapy and
getting away from my home. No, it was not the year off I imagined.
Certainly this was not the dream sabbatical I planned. That year was
more like a bump on the head, a wake-up call, a struggle sandwich.
But once the healing began, a new life would begin for me. Like a

ad emerged from its cocoon, I knew I could not go
ever go back to the work I excelled at, the home I
longer abuse my body with too much work or too
. I could no longer shut out my intuition, ignore my
soul, or deny my passion.

The reality is that I had been a writer since childhood. I majored
in English Literature in college, working for the school paper and
then later for a free press in Northern California. Poems in my 20's
and 30's gave way to short stories, and by the time I hit forty I was
writing novels … all on the road, while working my 'real' job. Too
busy to publish but too smart not to digitize, I had a body of work to
go along with my writing obsession. For decades, my friends and relatives had been receiving with enthusiasm my specially crafted
letters, post cards, or e-mails and whispering, "Why aren't you writing?" Why indeed.It took, finally, a sabbatical, being shaken to my
core and silenced by pain, to finally see. It took listening to strangers,
taking time, facing anxiety and restlessness, and fourteen months
traveling the globe for fourteen months, seeking a new home. But
through all of this, through healing and through grace, I found my
way back to my life's passion. Stumbling into my future, I made a
mid-life correction, heard a calling, and finally found my safe haven,
my soft landing. I picked up my pen and wrote.

~ Karen Jefferey

Inner Guidance

My life was full, yet something was missing. Along with being the mother of four healthy sons, I owned my own health food store. But in my marriage, my spouse and I were struggling with relating, and our attempts resulted in power struggles resembling war. I turned to prayer for guidance. I knew there was more purpose to my life, and I wanted to find what that was!

One afternoon I watched from the window as my husband walked around the yard. As he entered the house, his body was bent over in a 90-degree angle. It appeared he carried a heavy load. "Would you like me to massage your shoulders?" I asked. I knew nothing about massage techniques, and he never responded well to this kind of touch, so I was surprised when he said, "Yes. That would be nice."

He sat on a chair in the kitchen and rested his body on the table in front of him. As my hands worked, to my surprise, I felt an energy travel up my left arm and into my heart area. As the energy entered me, my partner's back began to straighten while at the same time I felt the pressure in my heart increasing. By the time he was upright, the pressure had built to where I felt I would burst at any moment! I had no idea what was going on, and in desperation called out in my thoughts to an unknown source, "I don't know what is happening. I don't know what to do. I feel like I will burst if I continue." At that moment a masculine voice from inside yet outside me at the same time said pointedly, "That is his pain, and his to deal with."

Instantly I withdrew my hands and with the force of a lightening bolt, the energy surged back to my husband, throwing him forward and triggering a huge emotional catharsis. The next moment and for a few hours that followed, my stoic friend sobbed!

The experience was my introduction to the connection between the body and emotions. I had been seeking a new direction in my career, and the universe was answering me, showing me my next step.

In an effort to learn more, I pursued studies in psychotherapy and then explored energy work. Healing became a passion. But in order to be a better instrument, I had to explore my own issues. As I went through my own inner healing process, I grew in understanding and awareness about how the body communicates to us. I learned ways to befriend pain, to explore it and listen to the messages it had to share.

I had many opportunities to witness the miraculous power of the mind and body to heal themselves. After I'd completed my learning, I joined a team of therapists who were assigned to work with a little girl with autism.

During one session, the child I was working with was particularly irritable. Suddenly, for no apparent reason, she began to shriek hysterically. I used all my skills to try to sooth her, but she continued to scream in apparent agony, backing herself against a wall, her cries full of pain.

Autistic children can be hypersensitive to stimulation, but this was extreme, to the point that even tiny movements such as breathing caused her to react. Searching within for guidance, I became very still, slowing my breath with focused effort. Finally she quieted down somewhat and for a moment our eyes met. I whispered ever so gently, "I want to help you," then carefully and very slowly inched my way toward her.

As I slid beside her, one hand instinctively reached for her jaw, and the other for her upper chest. I could instantly feel an energy gathered in her jaw like a balloon filled to the point of bursting.

Within the energy was also so much unexpressed emotion. No wonder the little girl was in so much agony! As I held her jaw, she slowly began to relax until she sank to the floor.

I began to doubt myself and wondered if what I was doing was wrong. With that thought, I withdrew my hands. She immediately grabbed my hands and with deliberate effort, placed them back into position! The little girl became my guide. When the energy released and balanced, she slipped off to sleep and later when she awoke, she was at peace.

Since that time, I've had many opportunities to practice listening to my inner guidance. I've learned to trust the unorthodox ways I'm sometimes led to use in the healing work I do. I have learned that if we accept pain as a friend who is showing us what we need to pay attention to, it will guide the way to health.

I have also learned it isn't up to me to heal another. In fact, I believe I don't have that capability. All any healer can do is offer assistance. Acceptance and love opens the door to receiving the guidance that is available to each of us, at all times!

~ *Deborah Maltman*

2

Getting to What's Important

Somewhere in your life there will be an overriding
theme to your quest—some part of your desire that
cannot be denied without a terrible cost to the very
essence of what you are. Are you going to ignore it,
or do you have the courage of your commitment and
the confidence to demand that life, humanity,
or circumstances give you what you want,
with no other excuse, reason or apology
other than that you demand it?

— Stuart Wilde

Entertaining Angels

Everyone has been made for some particular work, and
the desire for that work has been put in every heart.
— Jalaluddin Rumi

That morning I pulled into my usual parking space at the store where
I worked. What *wasn't* usual was my state of mind. I was distracted
and downhearted, still mulling over the disturbing news my boss had
dropped on me the day before:

> *"I've sold The Turquoise Shoppe ... the sale will be final at
> the end of the month. I'm sorry, but the new owner won't be
> needing you."*

That day it was my turn to open up the store. My mind drifted
as I dug for the keys that had sunk to the bottom of my favorite red
and black hand-woven Navajo purse. Purchasing beautiful Native
American handcrafts at an employee's discount was just one of the
many perks of working at the Shoppe. I had also enjoyed the interesting customers, the fair wages, and the free hand the owner gave me
as store manager. I would truly miss my job.

The news once again stirred up questions I had seemingly asked
too often in my life. What would I do next? What was I supposed to
BE when I grew up? My husband's work had required our family to
move many times over the course of our marriage, and I had devel-

oped the pattern of finding work that fit in with our family's needs. My resume was varied and full of short-term jobs. Two years here and three years there … there seemed to be no pattern to the jobs I would find myself in.

I genuinely enjoyed the variety I had experienced as a "Jill" of all trades. But still, each time I had to start over, I would feel a twinge of envy toward women who had a career, those confident ladies who could identify themselves as teacher or counselor or therapist. Was there something more important and specific I was *supposed* to be doing? Did God have a plan for me that I had somehow overlooked?

I shook off my melancholy thoughts, found the key, and put it in the lock. The door was balky as usual, but after a moment I was able to open it and flip the "Closed" sign in the window over to "Open." That was the last normal thing that happened …

How does one describe a vision? If that's what it *was*, for I have never had one before or since. As soon as I shut the door behind me, before I even had a chance to turn on the store lights, I realized the all-star cast of the long-canceled television show *Touched By An Angel* was in the room with me!

The unmistakable Della Reese, or rather Head Angel Tess, was waiting behind the cash register, smiling her dazzling, generous smile. By her side stood sweet Monica, the earnest Irish Apprentice, and Andrew, the kind and handsome Angel of Death! I stood dumbstruck, the keys dangling from my fingers. Later I would realize I had dropped my purse with a thud, the contents spilling at my feet.

Just like in many episodes from the popular series, not a word was spoken aloud by the "Angels." As their bodies radiated Golden-White Light, they silently and instantaneously conveyed the message that I was indeed doing exactly what God had planned for me. My nomadic life was no accident. Every temporary job, every move, every stop and start, each moment of my life's journey had a purpose. I was shown that I had connected in meaningful ways with hundreds of people while living in ten different states and one foreign country. Even though I had no awareness of it at the time, God's plan was well served by my wanderings.

The experience was both humbling and numinous. One minute the store was full of celebrity angels, and the next moment I was alone, an incredible sense of wonder and well-being filling my heart. With it dawned an appreciation of the daily service I can give in this lifetime. Those nagging questions about my purpose have been replaced with understanding. And my foot-dragging when I must face a new challenge has given way to an eagerness to discover what opportunities lie beyond the next bend.

~ Susan Higgins

Where the Truth Lies

It is not necessary to seek God, because God is already the essence of who you are. Simply remove all judgments and thoughts that do not bless you and others. Then the veil will be lifted and only God will remain.

— Paul Ferrini

I was going through a drought financially and wondering if I should leave the film industry altogether because of the stress caused by uncertainty in my line of work. Since 1984 I'd worked as a professional actor, experiencing only sporadic success. In the past years I'd appeared in numerous movies and four different TV series as a regular, and I had guest starred in Movies of the Week and TV series, but lately work had been very scarce.

In fact, it had gotten so sparse that I was scared I wouldn't be able to pay my rent or other bills. Normally I'm a high-energy person who tends to get involved in a flurry of projects. But this time I knew that to turn things around, the challenge would be to remain still. I realized that panicking or complaining would shut down my inner connection to Spirit when I needed this guidance the most. As a long-time student of spiritual teachings, I knew that to change my life I needed to keep my heart open to God 24/7. That way I wouldn't miss any messages or opportunities to change the landscape of my circumstance.

Remembering that the world without is a reflection of the world within, I decided against going out and running around, trying to drum up work in my usual fashion. I needed to go inward, slow down, and keep an attitude of gratitude. I began a mental fast, keeping my mind clear of any negative thoughts, words, and attitudes. Of course, this meant no complaining! I wanted my vibration to be receptive to love; my heart always open to my Inner Guidance.

Two days later I got a call from my agent. He told me that I had been cast in an Atom Eyogen film called *Where the Truth Lies*. The title jumped out at me like a waking dream; clearly this was all part of my conversation with God. Even more miraculous was the fact that I didn't have to audition because they'd cast me from my demo tape. The role allowed me to improvise my reactions (I could say whatever I felt like) to a comedy act performed by actors Kevin Bacon and Colin Ferth, who portrayed top comedians in the 1950s who were performing at a polio telethon and in a later scene, at a mafia club.

While on set, I continued my fast and did a spiritual exercise in which I imagined myself standing in a column of God's Light and Sound while Divine Love radiated through me.

Interesting things began to occur during this 14-hour day. Each time Kevin and Colin went through their routine, I laughed in my usual way-too-wild and unabashed style. My mother has always said that my laugh was unladylike. She often says, "Why you laughin' like Virago?" in her Jamaican accent. Virago is an old English word that means a shrewish Amazon woman. In other words, my mom thought I sounded like a hooligan.

After the first few hours on set, the first assistant director came up to me with thankful eyes and said, "You're bringing Spirit into the room. If it wasn't for you, everyone would just be just tittering, but your laughter is so contagious it's leading everyone into true laughter."

I was even more blown away when both Kevin and Colin

approached me and thanked me as well. They said that my laughter had helped them tremendously to feel more like the comedians they were portraying. Up until now it had been extremely difficult for them because neither found the material funny. Many others on set came over to tell me of their amazement that I could laugh for 14 hours without dropping my energy. I guess they didn't know that as part of my fast I was doing everything that day for God.

The day following the two-day shoot, I flew to Winnipeg, Canada, to speak and perform at a spiritual seminar entitled, "Wake Up to the Call of Soul." I volunteered my time and talents at this seminar, and it was a wonderful way to give back to Spirit. But I got a pleasant surprise when my agent called again, asking me to come home on an earlier flight because the producers wanted to hire me for another three days on the movie!

I went home on the next flight and back to work the next day. This time we were filming the polio telethon scene with 500 background extras on set. Extras are actors who are paid to fill in scenes on films by being passersbys or pedestrians, or in this case, audience members. I came back to the set still holding my thoughts on God. At one point before a scene, the first assistant director summoned me to stand. He instructed all the background actors to follow what I was doing as if I were the official 'Laugh Conductor.' It was quite comical how he introduced me almost like I was a savior about to lead the masses, saying "She has come; She knows The Way of Laughter; Do only as she does, and we shall win on this sacred day."

Something very infectious was catching on as one after the other, people approached me asking, "How do you laugh non-stop all day long?" or to say things like, "I heard you were auditioned for your laugh." I almost burst out laughing again when one person said, "I heard you are a professional laugher," or "You were hired as a professional laugher, right?" I thought, 'This is a first—a job where one gets paid to laugh.' As the day progressed, everyone on set was calling me the Laughing Lady.

When the job finally wrapped up, I had discovered some amazing things. By doing all things in God's name, I stumbled upon a profound truth: Laughter is a gift from God that can't be withheld. The more I laughed, the more I healed, and the more others were healed and able to fulfill their roles as servants of God. I have played many roles in my life, but I doubt I will ever be able to top the job of "official laugher."

~ Suzanne Coy

Don't Let Rejection Stop You!

The universe will pay you to be yourself
and do what you really love.
— Shakti Gawain

The journey to success can sometimes be very discouraging, and sometimes we are tempted to pick up all our toys and go home when the going gets a little rough. I certainly experienced that feeling many times in my attempt to become a published writer, but I pursued and pursued until I ultimately achieved success.

A little background: For many years, I had tried to sell my very first book, which I titled, *Feel the Fear And Do It Anyway*. After many, many rejections from just as many publishers, I woefully put the book proposal into a drawer and went on with my life.

Three years passed. One day I was going through the contents of the very same drawer that housed my sadly rejected and long-forgotten first attempt at a writing career. I picked my book proposal up … looked at it … paged through it … and all of a sudden, I was struck with the powerful sense that I held something in my hands that would be of help to many people. And, once again, but this time with a very strong resolve, I set out to find an agent and a publisher who believed in my book the same way I did. And this time, I succeeded. What's more, I succeeded beyond my wildest dreams.

I thought it would give you some encouragement if I shared

with you parts of the rejection letters that my wonderfully patient agent, Dominick Abel (three other agents had given up on me!) received from publishers to whom he submitted the book proposal for *Feel the Fear And Do It Anyway*. They may give you hope in your quest for success in whatever arena you choose to pursue … and a laugh or two. Naturally, I won't name the editors who wrote these comments … even the best are sometimes wrong. (That's an important thing to remember.) So, here they are … just a few of the many!

"I don't think that Susan Jeffers is ready yet for a book publication. I like her writing, I like her enthusiasm and, of course, I always celebrate change. The supporting material is thin as it stands, and she has not yet attained the visibility to sell her book in the national market. This material may lend itself to an article but certainly not a book. I'm sorry, but it's not for me now."

"Although I see the merit in this idea, I'm just not turned on by her writing."

"There's been a glut of self-help books in the last few years, and our figures indicate that the sales in this area are down considerably. To take on a book in this category, it would have to be almost revolutionary, and I didn't feel that way about this proposal."

"Thanks very much for letting us consider Susan Jeffers' proposal for *Feel the Fear And Do It Anyway*. It's quite nicely done. But my colleagues aren't enthusiastic about the commercial appeal of the subject itself and think we'd have a difficult time selling the book."

"This is an exceptionally strong proposal, but it's in a field which we unfortunately feel is glutted. Susan Jeffers is a savvy, articulate writer, and this book has a lot of good stuff in it. Her approach may even be utterly original—but the sense here is that it won't work in this glutted market."

"We will not be bidding on this book. We feel that there is too much competition now out there for this book, and it'll be an uphill battle to sell this book."

And the best rejection of them all . . .

"Lady Di could be bicycling nude down the street giving this book away and no one would read it."

You can see why I wanted to pick up my toys and go home. Thankfully, I didn't … nor did Dominick! He stuck with me and ultimately we made the first sale to Harcourt Brace Jovanovich. A wonderful editor there named Martha Lawrence (who now is the author of delightful mystery novels) saw the value in the book and bought it. The rest is history, as they say: After YEARS of trying, *Feel the Fear And Do It Anyway* was finally published in 1987. It has now sold millions and millions of copies and is presently available in over 100 countries and has been translated into over 35 languages. And these figures are growing every day.

I have received mail from all over the world with thanks for the words that I wrote. It seems that reading this book has helped so many people in so many ways. Some credited it with actually saving their lives. Wow! Thank goodness for that precious moment in time when I had the inner "knowing" that this book would make a difference in people's lives.

So in the world according to Susan Jeffers, when you have a dream, don't give up. While you may be rejected, those who are doing the rejecting may not know what a treasure they are holding in the palm of their hand. As long as YOU know in the depth of your heart that you have something wonderful to offer this world, in whatever form that is, you will have persistence … and a much greater chance of making your dreams come true.

So FEEL THE FEAR AND DO IT ANYWAY … and if it doesn't work one way, try another … and another … and another. Keep exploring. See where your efforts lead you. Be open to new experiences. The possibilities are limitless!

~ *Susan Jeffers*, Ph.D., from *Life is Huge!*

Pay it Forward

The remarkable thing is we have a choice every day
regarding the attitude we will embrace for that day. We
cannot change our past...we cannot change the fact that
people will act in a certain way. We cannot change the
inevitable. The only thing we can do is play on the one string
we have, and that is our attitude...I am convinced that life is
10% what happens to me and 90% how I react to it.

— Charles Swindoll

Growing up in a family of nine children, there were no extras to go around. My father worked long hours and frequently left my mom at home to raise us. I remember her crying when my father would leave because the many pressures of feeding and clothing our growing family placed significant stress upon her ultra-busy existence. But I also remember that no matter what our situation was, she would often attend to someone in need. Whether it was a hospital visit with flowers, a well-timed card, a phone call, or attention to someone else's circumstance, she seemingly willed the resources required. My mother always reiterated how important it was to give, and she demonstrated her values by stretching her few remaining dollars to soften someone else's experience.

As I grew, I observed that my mother was typically happy, and she appeared to have everything she needed. This combination was powerful in molding our family into balanced and generally happy individuals.

Like my mother, I made it a habit to give of myself, but I never did it to get something back. I just gave for the pure love and joy of serving. At 21, I married my high school sweetheart. We were very happy and went on to have three beautiful boys.

As our children grew, I noticed that my giving began to rub off on them. It began when Mitchell, then 13, asked me to drive him to the flower store on his lunch break so that he could buy roses for his girlfriend. He had seen me taking flowers to my friends over the years and had seen how my life was improved by the giving. My oldest son Robert frequently gave to street people because he had seen me do it.

As my kids grew, I longed to be back in the workforce, but I had no idea what I wanted to do. I had an earned a degree in nutrition while in university and had worked in the field somewhat, but I had been raising my children for the last 20 years. Now I was ready for my special mission. One day a close friend asked me the question, "What do you love more than anything else in the world, that you would be willing to do for free?" That was a no-brainer. I'd always wanted to help people.

Through a series of coincidences, I found my passion and at 46 went back to school to earn another degree as a Holistic Practitioner. When I opened my practice, I marveled at what happened. In less than one year, I managed to get myself on a local TV show that aired my story for six minutes. I just went to share my knowledge with no expectations about what I might receive in return. However, from that one show I received over 200 emails and literally hundreds of phone calls. The television station went crazy trying to field all the calls. For the next few days, my husband stayed home to answer the phone and to fill in my appointment calendar. I was booked four months in advance, and I hadn't even graduated yet!

The station asked me to return again for a second interview. Again the phone rang for weeks afterward. My email box was so full I could hardly keep up with the appointments and calls. Soon afterward I received an invitation by four other stations to participate in one of their programs as well. A full year later, I was still receiving calls from viewers who'd seen me and saved my number and email for a future date.

One day in the winter of 2004, one of my clients asked me if I could help out with a magazine promotion. The story chronicled two women's makeovers as they embarked on a health and wellness program for a number of months before each of them was to be married. I spent several days with them, enjoying the photo shoots and working with their health and dietary concerns. Money was never discussed, as I was volunteering my time. A week after publication of the story, a check arrived in the mail. I was flabbergasted. I simply never expected a reward!

I often wondered why I'd become so successful. But then I saw the relationship between success and giving. Just like my mother, I gave that last five dollars and took the time to send a card to someone I appreciated. Whether it was a free session, free sample, or staying beyond the length of an appointment, I would follow through. It did not matter if the session was free or full fee, I always gave 100%. People thanked me over and over for taking the time and making them feel that they were the most important person in the world. This was easy for me, since I honestly believed they were. I encouraged them, held their hands, and treated them as friends.

From word of mouth, I drew clients from all over Canada, the US, and even parts of Europe. My colleagues were amazed at my success. They just could not figure out why I was doing so well when we had the same education. It's love, I told them. Do it for love, or don't do it at all.

I was intrigued one day when my client told me he would drop off a powerful new supplement for me to try. The cost was $30.00. I paid him, and he told me he would deliver it the next day. While I was in session, my assistant received the package. Attached to it was a card that said, "Pay it forward" with the $30.00 inside. Although my finances were lean at that time, I knew that I was not to keep it, but give it to my assistant. She was shocked, but every muscle in my body knew that I needed to give the money away.

Over the years we have had our financial challenges, and many times I could not afford to do things that were necessary, but I always heard my mother's voice saying, "Give, even if it's your last few dollars."

The more you pay it forward, the more life pays it back. Sometimes I am amazed at the wonder of it all. At my recent graduation, I was nominated as valedictorian. I left them with my final secret: Be Love and Serve Life!

~ *Jane Durst-Pulkys*

Time is a Gift

To see the world in a grain of sand
and heaven in a wildflower
hold infinity
in the palm of your hand
and eternity in an hour.
— William Blake

Wednesday was a typical day. Running late on deadlines, I rushed more and more as the hands on the clock continued to move in a forward direction. I needed to get to the bank to do a deposit. There would be cheques going through the next day, and I needed to be sure the money was in the account before 3 p.m.

Finally, after the last of my morning phone calls, I picked up my wallet, car keys, and cell phone, and I headed to the car.

What a great day! The sun was shining brightly, and the air felt clean and fresh. I took a long, deep breath and relaxed for a few minutes, alone in my car, where no one could reach me. I had rushed so much that morning that I didn't even bother to break the speed limit getting to my destiny. Such leisure—if only for forty-five minutes.

I arrived at the bank just before noon. I had forgotten my deposit book, so I walked over to the island to fill in a deposit slip. In my mind I was a thousand miles away from everything. I reached to take a deposit slip from its tray when all of a sudden a voice yelled out, "Everybody down on the floor." I looked up. There stood a person on the other side of the banking counter dressed in a dark sweatshirt, holding a gun in his hand.

I stood there looking at them. Then I smiled to myself. Cute. This was noontime entertainment. He was a good actor, but he sure wouldn't get an Academy Award for this performance. There was another customer in the bank standing at the teller wicket directly in front of this person. He stood looking at the gunman silently.

Again the voice rang out, "Everyone down on the floor!"

I just stood there looking at him eye-to-eye. I couldn't make out the face or any features. This was most unusual. However, I looked at the gun a little more seriously—it was a shiny silver revolver. He shouted, "Open the drawer, open the second drawer, hurry up! Quit stalling!" He then looked at the other customer and myself and roared, "Everybody down the floor, NOW!"

Suddenly it registered—This person is serious! Faster than I could faint, I was lying face down on the floor of the bank, terrified.

It's amazing the thoughts that go through one's mind in these situations. Lying on the floor, all I could think was "I'm the closest person to the door when this guy leaves, so please don't anyone aggravate him." Scenario One: He could shoot me in the back. That would hurt, maybe permanently. Scenario Two: He could drag me out of the bank as a hostage. Who would tell my children? What would happen to them? No matter what I thought, I could only pray that he would leave the bank by himself with everyone inside still alive.

The second thought that went through my mind was "Please don't take my wallet." When he had said for the third time, "Get down on the floor!" I did just that, leaving my wallet and a cheque sitting on the island counter. Inside my wallet were three one hundred dollar bills. What would happen if he took those—who would replace them? What strange thoughts went through my mind!

He left the bank as fast as he had entered it, hurdling over the counter. The other customer who was in the bank ran out and jumped into a car that was waiting for her. They followed the bank robber, but he was soon out of sight. The police arrived and took everyone's statement. I was then allowed to leave.

Thankfully, everyone was alive and well, but very shook up.

A couple of hours later I was sitting in my front yard. My reaction to the event was 'Stop the world! I want to get off!' As a successful, self-employed, single mother of three teenagers, I really had to stop and ask myself, Why was I working so hard? Why was I allowing myself to miss all the things in life that mattered most? Why did I continually rush, rush, rush, trying to please everyone, striving to be the best, for people who really mattered the least in my life? No one in the bank was more important than the other, especially to the guy with the gun in his hand.

My second reaction to this event was that time no longer seemed to exist. It had come to a complete stop. I didn't know what day or week it was for quite a while. Funny, when I look back, I see that I had been so time conscious before, but then time just seemed to stop. Was there a lesson here for me?

Savor time.

Since then, I have moved from the rush and chaos of the city to the peacefulness of the country. I enjoy the morning sunrise and the evening sunset. I watch the storms move across the hills as they shed their rain. I cherish the moment. There is no alarm clock to wake me up in the mornings, and strangely enough, I wake up more easily and earlier now than when I used to set an alarm every day.

Today, I still have unrealistic deadlines to meet, but one thing has become quite clear to me since then. The law of nature, the universe, whatever you may choose to call it, has its own clock that applies to everything and everyone. I can't alter the timing that has been set in motion for me. As hard as I might try, seldom does an event, or my work, turn out to be what I expected. Instead, I find that life unfolds in its own way, and in its own time.

~ *Karen Thomas Petherick*

Before You

For my daughter Melanie

Before you
There was Washington, D.C.:
The crisp click of high-heeled shoes
In gleaming subway stations,
A window office overlooking the Potomac.
Next to you, empty
As a cellophane box.

Before you
There were stylish business suits
And cocktail parties,
Committee meetings, and bound reports.
One little giggle
Makes them all laughable.

Before you
There were reams of academic research,
Published papers, and names on programs.
One dimpled grin
Turns them all to dust.

Before you,
Everything mattered so much,
And came to so little.
Now nothing seems to matter much at all anymore
Compared to you.

~ *Laura Reave*

Employed By Love

Sometimes life's shadows are caused
by our standing in our own sunshine.
— Ralph Waldo Emerson

I lost God on the summit of Mount Sinai in May 1985. In a small group, my cousin and I climbed up the goat path in 52 degree centigrade dry heat. Completely unprepared when the temperature dropped to 6 degrees, I shivered sleepless throughout that long night. The energy of the mountain felt alarmingly indifferent. Many intellectual debates on Divinity and mysticism at university had abstracted my faith into a concept of clever words until there was nothing left. That night I lost God as I'd been brought up to know God. To my dismay, when the full moon rose cold and distant over the expanse of grim mountains, it seemed all that was familiar to me was beyond reach. Feeling essentially alone on that holy mountain, I unwittingly experienced a spiritual crisis.

Sunrise finally came, warming us and shining golden on the temple built where the Burning Bush is believed to have stood. While descending, I began my inner journey to make the Divine more personal and accessible, to integrate my spirituality in order to prevent losing my compass again.

A year later, the shocking 1986 murder of Alison Parrott resulted in two immediate decisions that altered the course of my life. Enroute to a sales presentation, I heard the radio station reporting the death of this beautiful 11-year-old girl in Toronto. I don't know why her stolen life hit me so hard. Perhaps I identified with her young, enthusiastic, athletic spirit, and could imagine at that age being just as trusting and naive with a deceitful stranger. The empty, useless agenda of my day screamed its incongruity. At that moment I decided that my working life required more meaning. When my employer demonstrated a complete lack of compassion for my attendance at Alison's public memorial service, I chose to quit.

After Alison's memorial service, I accepted a sales job at a much larger company. There I met Bill Sheridan, a friend who profoundly shaped my healing and reeducation path. In 1988 he introduced me to the then little-known Usui Reiki. My emotional and spiritual healing began.

The following year Gestalt Therapy sessions complimented my personal growth process. I also impulsively bought a house for way too much money, without savings and with someone I didn't know very well, a crazy decision that taught me the demands of commitment. I rediscovered a resourcefulness I had forgotten I possessed.

My childhood training came back to bolster me in this time. My parents had emigrated from Egypt to Canada with three young children in 1965. Growing up in Ontario, we spent vacations pursuing adventures in the natural world: hiking, canoeing, and camping in the wilderness. My mother and father each went back to school to train in new careers while supporting the family. Witnessing their model of risk-taking, courage, and humor through adversity gave me the confidence and strength to pursue adventure and challenge in my own life.

For example, after impulsively joining a friend of my sister on a bicycle trip through the Canadian Rockies in 1990, she and I naively cycled up to Moraine Lake, Alberta. Two unexpected, grueling uphill hours later, we arrived at the extraordinary mountain vista illustrated on the back of older Canadian $20 bills. It was a destination I NEVER would have given myself credit for being strong enough to reach. Descending took a full 20 minutes of steady gliding, my hands cramping on the brakes, incredulous at my achievement all the way down the mountain.

Another invitation to adventure came soon after I bought my house, when my roommate and her new husband moved abroad. In 1991 he offered me a plane ticket to come visit. At the age of 18 I'd heard the melodic word Kathmandu and promised myself I'd go one day. Malaysia was close enough to Nepal; I seized this moment of invitation and took a leave of absence to realize that teenage dream.

On my stopovers in Bangkok, my transfer agent Sam took me through the congested, noisy roadways that led to the King's Palace, past buildings adorned with countless intricate, sparkling mosaics, to water markets spilling with fragrant, colorful wares. When Sam shared stories of the struggles and limitations of daily life in Thailand, I recognized that my ability to choose to educate myself, travel the world solo, change jobs, borrow money, buy real estate—these all were privileges I took for granted. The financial struggles of home ownership had made me identify with scarcity, but now I experienced an epiphany: I was indeed truly wealthy, confident, and free.

Trekking in Nepal brought me a rhythmic, tangible connection with the earth, unbridled by ceiling or walls, inspiring these verses:

> *Amidst this company of strangers*
> *We find Giants rise up from the mist*
> *This place once found only in dreamland*
> *Comes to life each morn with a kiss*
>
> *Of the sun as it warms every mountain*
> *And dries up the dew on the tents*
> *With the clear Sherpa song that leads us*
> *On a trail where 10,000 footsteps are spent.*

Within this company of strangers
Burns a bold shining new light
Born in the Great Himalaya
With our hopes, our dreams, and our might.

Mile-long, month-long philosophical discussions with the trek leader forged my commitment to train in psychotherapy upon my return. Back in Toronto, I enrolled in another adventure: a part-time training program at the Gestalt Institute. My final undergrad paper explored the relationship between Gestalt theory and Reiki's intuitive process. I applied the model to my modest private Reiki practice.

My artistic spirit was rekindled during the program, and I began painting playful, lusty images of fruits, expressing my deepening joy and gratitude for the beauty in the mundane. Tuition was covered by a series of sold-out solo exhibitions.

With Bill Sheridan's urging I discovered Therapeutic Art courses at Haliburton School of the Arts, which developed into an Expressive Arts Certificate taken over five summers on vacation time. My professor encouraged the Truly Madly Deeply Art and Therapy workshops I offered in my home studio in which I used Gestalt theory to process the creative exercises. Concurrently I was writing my Gestalt postgrad thesis. These workshops provided the clinical data that supported my argument for the effective healing combination of art and Gestalt therapy.

To celebrate my 40th birthday I embarked on a seven-day seakayaking excursion on Georgian Bay in 2000. Then that September my intuitive friend, Stavroula, asked me: *What would happen if I put all my passions—sea kayaking and adventure, healing, art, and nature—together to create a business that didn't yet exist? Could I create something that enables people to remember who they are?*

Recognition flowed through my body. I wept for the completeness of the vision, for this answer that I'd been seeking and unknowingly training for all these years. Luckily my mortgage had motivated me to remain full time in graphic arts sales and marketing, an invaluable 18-year investment towards this new business venture.

For 14 years I'd been juggling my day job while training in Reiki, Gestalt, and Expressive Arts. During the last 7 years I had facilitated workshops and retreats on weekends and vacations. The cosmic boot came when my biggest sales client went bankrupt. Without income from this 'secure' job, I thought, I might as well start my new business full time. Commissioned sales had seasoned me to financial uncertainty, but nothing could have prepared me for the challenges of the entrepreneurial journey ahead.

Before leaving graphic arts, I had a dream in which I was on a large boat with my mother, overlooking Greenland's shore. A tidal wave engulfed the vessel, and we were separated. Falling feet first into the silver, streaming trough of the wave, I sensed no evil. I woke up in a state of unrelenting free fall, and I have remained there ever since. An ending to the dream came to me while on the Reiki table: My fall slowed. Looking to see how I was able to control my landing I noticed I had grown wings. Still without visible ground under me, the surrounding wall of wave turned into a stadium filled with tiers of applauding angels encouraging my endeavor to fly.

Aziza Healing Adventures was announced to friends and family in 2001. In Arabic, Aziza is an endearment meaning "beloved, cherished one." It means invincible. Aziza is also a benevolent African Faerie race that bestows practical and spiritual knowledge on humans. And Aziza Healing Adventures abbreviates to AHA, a Gestalt term describing sudden insight.

I had created a new lifestyle, rather than a job: 5 p.m., Fridays, vacations and retirement would no longer punctuate my lifeline. I became a traveling therapist. However, the tragedy of 9/11 postponed my first season's scheduled retreats and provoked doubts about initiating an international personal growth company at such a time of loss and global unrest. My ambition seemed frivolous, and I was deeply discouraged. Friends consistently countered that this healing initiative was needed now more than ever.

So I built it, and they came. I was given a beautifully designed 10-page web site, and people from around the world who were seeking self-discovery found it. Women and men came to experience an adventure: to discover who they are outside the roles that dictate their daily norm; to remember that they have a creative, emotional, and physical life; to reconnect to this gorgeous planet in sacred and special places; to be aware; to live authentically. It seems to be working.

I'm now employed by Love. The tragedy of 9/11 brought a sobering awareness of the diligence required to attend to residual bitterness and blame. It raised the bar towards impeccable leadership. It led me to insist on combating the fear that clips my wings and would have me cling to the illusion of safety and security, challenging me away from the comfortable known of home, asking me to grow into the beckoning unknown. Love invites me to trust the free fall. A meaningful life takes on many forms, and I thank God each day that this calling chose me.

~ *Laila Ghattas*

My Invisible Hands

I worked only for big name companies. I traveled regularly to exciting cities such as San Francisco, New York, and Berlin, interacting with celebrities such as Pelé, the greatest soccer player of all time. I had been honored at recognition events in Hawaii and Palm Springs. But after 18 years, I found myself staring at my watch in sheer boredom and sneaking out during lunch hours to dusty yet enchanting horse stables to volunteer my time in horse therapy programs. I had an itch to leave my corporate life, but I didn't have the guts. I prayed for a severance package, and on a beautiful, chilly day in late April, my prayers were answered. "There has been a restructuring, and your position has been eliminated. Thank you for your nine years of service," said my manager by phone, reading the words from a carefully crafted script written by Human Resources.

This was the moment I had been waiting for. I now had permission to pursue whatever it was I was going to do with the rest of my life. I was excited about the future and confident that something wonderful and fulfilling was going to take place. So what was I going to do next? An idea quickly popped into my head, and off I went to visit the animal shelter and comfort the cute faces I'd seen on the Internet.

The property was rustic, with two small brick buildings surrounded by a chain-link fence. As I was getting ready to leave, I tried to unlock the fence leading to the dirt road where I entered, but it was locked. I entered the building closest to the parking lot to find a detour. There I followed a dark and narrow hallway that led to a conference room with a big window where I could see several women. I decided to enter the room and ask for directions out of the property. The women instead focused on my orange tennis racquet key chain and asked, "Do you play tennis?" to which I answered "Yes." They next asked me if I had a few minutes to sit down and join them. I laughed to myself because little did they know I had all the time in the world!

I learned that this was a planning meeting for a charity tennis tournament. The goal was to raise money for the animal shelter, and they wanted me to be on the committee. Within 90 minutes of losing my job, I had been led to an exciting opportunity that tapped into some of my favorite passions: animals, tennis, and event planning! A higher power must have led me to that conference room. Immediately, I was involved in something meaningful, and I knew something even bigger and better was in store.

In addition to planning the event, I spent the summer evaluating myself to determine what my next vocation was going to be. I took assessments, journaled, job shadowed with the elephant keepers at the zoo, interviewed for corporate positions with no enthusiasm, read self-discovery books, and listened to my heart. I decided I was going to talk to career coaches and learn more about their profession, seek their advice, develop contacts, and find a position as an outplacement consultant. After all, I had helped family and staff members advance their careers all my life!

I remember my first morning in outplacement. It was 6:30 a.m., pitch black, and I was on my way to a company that was downsizing 200 unsuspecting employees within two hours. A full moon shone immaculately on the road ahead of me. It captivated me so completely that I almost drove off the road! I'd never seen such brilliance in the wee morning hours. It was a sign that I was on the path to something extraordinary in my life. From that moment, the magic began, and invisible hands led me on a path full of purpose.

In a short period of time, I was the most sought-after career consultant at the firm. I began coaching other consultants as they were between jobs themselves. *The Wall Street Journal* began calling me for their Career Journal section of the paper. They looked to me for story ideas, trends, quotes, resources, and contacts. I was onto something big here. *The Wall Street Journal* thought of me as an expert, and so I decided to dedicate my life to becoming one.

Soon after, an editor at McGraw-Hill publishing in New York phoned to ask me if I'd like to write a book. Her job was to seek out new authors, and she read *The Wall Street Journal* for this purpose. Most writers struggle for years to get a major book deal, yet here I was being offered a deal I hadn't even sought! Then even more offers came in. *The Atlanta Journal-Constitution* asked me to write a career column, and my articles began showing up in international and domestic magazines. Finally, I left the outplacement firm to start my own career-coaching and resume-writing business. The clients kept coming—nationwide!

I had found my calling, and life was good. But what I've since learned is that life doesn't stand still. Every day we must adjust our activities, goals, and purpose as the world changes around us. I've been sent people who really need help and who are emotionally distressed. I've also been sent opportunities in pet therapy to promote physical, spiritual, and emotional healing to those in need. All of a sudden I'm attracting animals into my life, ways to work with them to help human beings in need, and new clients that need much more than just job leads, career help, and a sparkling new resume.

I trust that the invisible hands will continue to navigate me through the many storms and opportunities of life, and in the end, they will help me find individuals that desperately need the kind of help I can provide. I have total confidence in the process, and I know I can never stand still.

~ *Lori Davila*

3

Healing to Move Ahead

Until you make peace with who you are,
you'll never be content with what you have.

— Doris Mortman

From an Ocean of Tears a Universe of Possibility

*One can have no smaller or greater mastery
than mastery of oneself.*
— Leonardo da Vinci

Every day after I arrived in Aceh, the northern-most province of Sumatra, the area hardest hit by the December 26 tsunami, was full of profound and moving events, including feeling the earth shake beneath my feet during a second massive earthquake.

Sumatra has coal, oil, and natural gas in abundance, making control of these assets a matter of great economic importance. For centuries, the Achenese have been revolting against the Dutch, Portuguese, Japanese, and now the Indonesian government. Aceh was still under martial law and closed to foreigners when a massive earthquake of 9.0 on the Richter scale triggered the tsunami. Traveling at 800 km per hour, that monster wall of water slammed into the coast, creating a wave of unimaginable destruction and death. The highest death toll was in Aceh, where an estimated 200,000 died and 400,000 were left homeless.

Our small medical team consisted of myself, a general practitioner who specializes in women's health and alternative medicine; Harvest, a midwife and self-taught herbalist and healer; Eda, a fantastic Balinese chef, former restaurant owner and translator; and

Eric, a Dutch house builder who had lived in Bali for the last 16 years and who spoke five languages.

Three months post tsunami, we arrived by plane to Medan, the capital of Sumatra, and hitched a ride on a Red Cross plane to the coastal city of Meulobah in Aceh province. Our team was sponsored by two Indonesian-based NGOs: IDEP (Indonesian Development of Education and Permaculture) and WAHLI (Wahana Lingkungan Hidup Indonesia), as well as the Balinese midwife clinic called Bumi Seaht, (The Good Earth), founded by American pioneer, poet, and author Robin Lim.

Three quarters of the people and the buildings of Meulobah were completely wiped out. Meulobah and Banda Aceh, and the whole 300 kilometer coastline in between, bore the full brunt of the tsunami. Entering Meulobah, I was shocked at the devastation, but I also saw that the city was starting to come back to life. Motor scooters were buzzing through the ruins, and the newly formed market was selling a good variety of fruits, vegetables, meat, and fish.

We were picked up and driven to the clinic, one hour from Meulobah. The clinic was on high ground, so it had suffered no tsunami damage. It was constructed out of local bamboo and trees. There was a spacious front porch where mats were spread out so it could be used as a gathering space for survivors as well as a waiting area for the clinic. Between 40 and 60 people visited every day for the morning and evening clinics.

Before arriving, I had been worried that I couldn't handle the enormity of the grief. I wasn't sure about my stability. In November of 2003 I had been through my own personal tsunami, when my partner of 24 years suddenly died of a heart attack.

Yet right from the beginning, I felt that I could do this. I felt at home as a practitioner of complementary or integrative medicine, combining the best of both worlds, natural and conventional. I loved the day-to-day challenge, the constantly changing situation, the innovative use of the limited supplies we had, and the creativity in our daily solving of practical problems for the Achenese people. I quickly realized I was getting back as much as I was giving.

Our mandate at the clinic was to be politically neutral as well as culturally and environmentally sensitive. We tried to be as low impact as possible, using remedies that people could still find locally long after the Western aid organizations had gone. We showed many people how to soak infected body parts in warm salt water. I trained people in how to clean out infected wounds with warm saline compresses. We also used local honey to draw infections out of wounds (Harvest's innovation).

In addition, we used high quality essential oils and many Chinese herbal remedies. Oregano oil was one of our standbys for all kinds of fungal-related skin problems. This we diluted and handed out in little plastic zip-lock bags with cotton balls soaked in the solution. We also used diluted tea tree oil. Harvest hauled large bottles of herbal tinctures across the Pacific Ocean. These remedies she had lovingly made from handpicked herbs in the Kootenays, in British Columbia, which is where we both live.

Almost from the first day, we documented the medicinal use of local herbs, and started to organize a garden to plant these herbs. One man arrived at the clinic with astronomically high blood pressure, and we had no medications available to treat him. The next day he came back looking much improved. He had been using the leaves of a local tree, and his blood pressure was back to normal. A tree with that leaf (starfruit) was growing a few meters from the clinic, and when recounting how to make this recipe for other patients who had high blood pressure, we could point at the tree. From another patient, we learned the herbs that were useful for diabetes. There were no drugs available for treating that condition. We used a powder from the turmeric family for liver ailments. Harvest showed two community midwives how to burn the umbilical cord, a simple and sustainable method pioneered by Robin Lim. This method of burning the umbilical cord prevented tetanus infection from the contaminated instruments that had been killing newborns.

Nonetheless, we never hesitated to use antibiotics, painkillers, or other drugs when these were absolutely necessary or when natural remedies didn't work, for example, for some ear, bladder, and kidney infections. There were many serious wound infections such as penicillin-resistant staphylococcus infections that required the use of antibiotics.

On the day of the second earthquake, we were all sitting out on the porch of our jungle clinic. All conversation stopped as we sat together to wait it out, praying that there would be no tsunami this time. The building swayed from side to side for almost seven minutes. I felt calm, knowing there was nothing I could do. Ibu Isa, our cook, was on one side chanting to Allah, while on the other side Eda was wailing to Jesus *and* Allah.

As soon as it was over, Hendra, our quiet handyman whose wife had been washed away by the tsunami, pointed to the road, which was now filled with people fleeing with all of their important possessions by motor scooter. The fear of a tsunami loomed large in everyone's minds. All the people we had visited on the weekend who had been celebrating the resettlement of their old village were now running for higher ground.

Shortly afterwards a messenger from the local mosque came to ask our help for a woman who had fainted. I jumped on a scooter with Ade, our Balinese community organizer, as the rain came down in torrents. I had my white coat on and a headscarf to go to the mosque. I was drenched to the skin when we arrived, took off our shoes and made our way to a woman who was lying flat on the ground. There were at least a hundred people gathered at the mosque. I quickly realized she was already dead. Ade had the difficult task of telling her son, who was a friend of his.

One day we saw a whole series of fishermen who had been on the ocean when the tsunami hit and somehow rode out the waves in their boats. Then they made their way to their villages to discover their homes flattened and their wives, children, mothers, and fathers gone. Many never found the bodies of their loved ones.

One young boy, with dark circles under his eyes and long, slender, cold fingers, was a walking shell, having lost his whole family. We used all our resources, our whole trauma treatment on him. Afterwards, every night he passed through the clinic he made eye contact with Eric and me; each time he stayed a little longer. And sometimes he smiled.

With no Western drugs available for depression or anxiety, we listened, we counseled, and we held hands. We saw the positive changes in people every day. Our founder Robin Lim called our tenure there 'a crash course in the religion of gratitude.'

Every day Eric would ask, "Waktu tsunami, di mana anda?"— Where were you during the tsunami? Then a series of questions began: "Is your house gone? Did you lose any family members? Did you run or did you swim? Where are you living now? How are you sleeping?"

The people continued to amaze us with their friendliness, their kindness, and their courage. It was never just another day at the clinic; there was always another surprise around the corner, another amazing adventure.

On the last day Eric and I went on a motor scooter to the beach. On either side of the highway were ruins produced by the tsunami —everything flattened or upended, the mostly concrete structures of homes and offices wiped out. The rebuilding would take a long time, years instead of months, and our secret hope was that in the rebuilding, there would be more sustainability and more respite from civil war.

Now most of the Indonesian army has finally left Ache. IDEP, one of our sponsoring groups, is now building a model permaculture village, with sustainable agriculture, craft workshops, and animal husbandry. They will also be starting a college to train the trainers who will go back to their small villages and teach what they have learned.

When I decided to come to Aceh, I was afraid I wouldn't be able to handle the immense losses that so many had experienced and the vastness of the grief suffered there. But the experience I found was more about life than death, more about hope than despair, more about resiliency rather than fragility. The brave, patient, and generous spirit of the Achenese people is what I will remember with great affection. The Achenese gave me a sense of how I could use all my experiences in a cohesive way, in another world far from my own, with people of very different nationalities, motivations, and religions. It opened my eyes to the macrocosm within the microcosm, the common grief about the human condition that we all share. It has opened me to a whole universe of possibility.

~ *Dr. Carolyn DeMarco*

Winter Fog

The white air this morning is so thick
There is only a vague line
Between the snow-covered field
And the snow-white sky.
Two white poles stand high
A reminder of games long past,
While on the roof birds scratch
At the chimney,
Searching for a warm place to hide.
But this is no home to them.
Whatever shelter they find,
Huddled inside the bushes and bare trees,
Is only to hold them until the time of green,
When rivers once frozen run free.

~ Laura Reave

The Right Words

Listening is a magnetic and strange thing, a creative
force ... When we are listened to, it creates us,
makes us unfold and expand. Ideas actually begin to
grow within us and come to life ... When we listen to
people there is an alternating current, and this
recharges us so that we never get tired of each
other ... and it is this little creative fountain inside us
that begins to spring and cast up new thoughts and
unexpected laughter and wisdom. ... Well, it is when
people really listen to us, with quiet fascinated
attention, that the little fountain begins to work
again, to accelerate in the most surprising way.
— Brenda Ueland

"Stop, Mom, don't do it. There's a car beside us!" I was about to
change lanes on a busy highway when my son called out the warning.
Looking over my left shoulder, I saw the vehicle in the space I had
intended to move into. My son constantly amazed me with his sense
of timing to deliver the right words at just the right time.

I look back at one incident and smile. Jason had been bouncing
his soccer ball off the wall after a neighbor had complained it was
irritating. Despite my warning, he was back at it again! Infuriated, I
began shouting at him to stop. But Jason, a 6 foot 2 muscular athlete,

walked over and with a huge smile, just picked me up. I tried to continue lecturing, but my anger had melted.

Another time, I'd been given a yellow hooded sweatshirt by the staff at a Catholic Separate School as a thank-you gift for teaching their students dance. When Jason saw the sweatshirt featuring the rival school's football team name and logo, he said, "I hope you're not planning on wearing that, Mom!"

"Why not? It's new and nice looking," I responded.

A few days later, I arrived home to find Jason wearing the hoodie. Surprised, I asked, "Surely you didn't wear that to school today?"

"Yes," he replied, "I did."

"Oh my goodness," I said, "What happened?"

"Well," he responded calmly, "they threw me up against the lockers and called me names."

I said, "Oh, Jason! I guess you won't be doing that again!"

"Why not, Mom? It builds character!" he said.

That same spring 1989, Jason was competing in the Western Canadian Track and Field competition. In the morning, he hugged me just before he left to drive to the event. All that day it felt as if everything were out of sync. It was just a wretched day. Later that evening when Jason hadn't returned home when he should have, I phoned the police. They assured me there were no car accident reports, but I couldn't shake the feeling that something was wrong.

An hour or so later a policeman came to the door. I could tell by his face something was very wrong. No words can describe my horror when in the next instant he delivered the terrible message that my son was dead. "No," I begged the officer. "He's really all right. He's just hurt. Take me to him. He's just hurt. Please tell me he's just hurt!" But the officer calmly told me that just an hour after Jason had given me his goodbye hug, he'd lost control of his car. Within minutes he was dead.

I was in a state of numbness. My reality was shattered. There would be no more balls bouncing against the walls, no more late night gabfests, no more shopping together at eleven at night for groceries. No more Jason.

I learned later from the people driving behind him that his car had suddenly veered out of control for no apparent reason. Later, our family doctor surmised that Jason must have suffered an aneurism. I never learned if it were true, for each time I tried filling in the request for the medical accident report, I wound up sobbing uncontrollably.

For the next several months I felt that I was in a dream. I was stunned, overwhelmed with such immense sorrow that I couldn't speak. For a long while, I didn't even recognize people I knew. I couldn't recall the names of friends I'd known for years.

I had no idea how I would go on. Three months after Jason's death, I stood in church surrounded by hundreds of people, observing a mother and son standing together in the crowd and feeling tortured at the realization that I would never hold my son again. Then suddenly Jason was standing beside me on my left. I could even smell his aftershave.

"You haven't lost me, Mom. I'm still here," he said.

Time stood still. There was no other sound. No movement. There was just my beloved seventeen-year-old. I felt such comfort for the first time since his death. And then I realized that what he said was true: Death hadn't separated us. The tie between us was still strong.

The following day I decided to test this connection. I said to him, "Jason, I can hardly wait until I die so we can be together again." Once again, I heard his voice so clearly, as though he was at a distance and had turned to speak to me. "You came to this earth with a plan," he said. "And there are unfinished tasks you still need to complete. Live for today."

I knew then I needed to honor Jason. That meant living my life in the present while cherishing the time we'd been given while he was here.

Something about my meeting with Jason must have started a divine agreement, because inexplicably over the next few weeks strangers began sharing their stories with me. They were true stories like my own, of a deceased loved one appearing to a grieving person with a message of consolation. At first I thought, "What a coincidence that all these people should bring me their stories!" I felt unworthy to think God might be orchestrating this experience for me. It didn't occur to me then that I might have a role to play in the healing of those who needed to tell their stories and later, for tens of thousands of readers who needed to hear them. Each time someone shared their story we cried together, and each time I healed a little more as I shared the story of Jason and his messages.

It was my husband, Shawn, who suggested I put the stories into a book that could offer people hope. Excited about the prospect, I began working on it. Then I stopped.

I was suddenly concerned about the rightness of what I was doing. Why didn't I just ask God? I think because I didn't have the faith that He would answer me. I put my energies back into my job as director of health, fitness and lifestyles for the local Y.M.C.A.

It was almost three years later, when I quit my job to write a children's book of rhymes, that I began to get signs to write a book of stories of heavenly intervention. One after another, eight times in all, I was shown that this was the right thing to do.

Writing the book became a healing journey for me, a four-year privileged task. I didn't advertise for stories, yet they came to me by the hundreds. It was as if I were suddenly a magnet for stories about angels, special dreams, deathbed visions, and after-death communication. I was to learn about realities that I never even imagined could be possible.

As I worked on the book, I yearned to hear my son's voice again. Five years after his death, I broke down sobbing and begging God, "Please, just let my son give me a hug in a dream?" That very week

I had a healing dream that taught me a deep lesson. In the dream Jason was seven or eight years old, measuring only up to my chest. I was reprimanding him for something and said emphatically, "Don't do that. You could get killed!"

He looked up at me innocently and said, "But, Mom, death isn't forever." Jason was showing me that death is an illusion!

I finally published my book of stories called *A Little Door, A Little Light* and was soon invited to speak at conferences and church meetings. Because of my fear of being ridiculed, I spoke only of the miraculous stories of others, and I kept my own story a secret. As an author I had published books on creative movement and some children's stories. After one event where I'd been speaking on my book on creative movement, people were gathered around a table where my books were displayed for sale. One lady picked up *A Little Door, A Little Light* and asked, "What's this one about?"

Her question caught me off guard. I swallowed, looking at the small group waiting expectantly. Apprehensively I began telling them of Jason, his death and his miraculous appearance in church. For a moment no one spoke. Then conversations resumed, purchases were made, and people left.

I was almost packed up and ready to leave when one of the ladies reappeared, tears streaming down her face. She choked on her words, fighting for control. "I just wanted to thank you for telling your story," she said. Then she told me how she'd seen her own child who'd passed away and how her family told her never to speak of it or they'd lock her up.

"Thank you, this has been like a gift to me," she said before she left. I knew then why I needed to share my words and the book.

When the book, *A Little Door, A Little Light*, was published, I looked back, marveling at the road I had traveled, grateful for the support of God and my husband. I thought my job was done, and I felt a little sad that I would no longer be collecting the beautiful stories. I was soon to learn this was not the finish.

One evening a friend telephoned me. Shari has special gift of working with energy to assist people in healing themselves. She began to speak, stuttered, started again, interrupted herself, and then beat around the bush to the point of frustration. Finally she said, "You're going to find this difficult to believe, but I received five messages from Jason. He wanted me to share them with you." What made this even stranger was that Shari had never met my son, as she had come into my life several years after his death. What's more, she had never had an experience with communicating with the dead, so the entire experience really shook her up.

It had been a long time since Jason had come to me, so I was awestruck by the fact that he'd been trying to get through and had resorted to contacting my friend Shari. I waited in anticipation for the words she had for me.

She told me Jason had said, "*Tell my mom not to go to Calgary tomorrow.*" I drew in my breath. I was planning the trip but had not discussed it with anyone. God alone knew my plans.

The next message had been, "*Tell my mom if she stays home she will get an important story.*" I stayed and I did. I received two stories that will be included in the new book.

The third message was more personal and puzzling. I did not understand it for months, but eventually it sunk in. He said, "*Tell my mom to talk to my dad.*" We had been divorced two years before Jason's death, and now Jason's father was living in the shadow of cancer. It turned out that he needed to discuss something with me regarding our daughters, and it was important that the lines of communication be open.

The fourth message, "*Tell my mom she should write another book. It will help ease the pain for others.*" It was just the right message because I knew it was something I had wanted to do. And of course God knew it too.

The final and fifth message was, "*Tell my mom I love her.*"

I was deeply touched by the messages from Jason and knew I needed to follow through with a sequel to *A Little Door, A Little Light.*

It has now been 16 years since Jason's death. People often write to me, especially those who have lost a child. They know I have walked the path they are just beginning. We talk. I speak to them like a big sister trying to help them along a tough road. I feel privileged to have these opportunities, and I am always amazed at the healing that takes place.

Isn't it all astounding?

~ *Ellie Braun-Haley*

Connecting to a Higher Purpose

Be the change you wish to see in the world...
— Gandhi

It was my father's birthday, August 2003. I had planned my afternoon to fit in a few minutes of downtime so I could call him in Canada, where he and the rest of my family lived, to wish him a happy birthday. At the time, I was working as a personal assistant in Los Angeles. After running a few errands, I decided to speed through some grocery shopping before I had to pick up my boss's kids and take them to their tennis lesson. There I'd have a spare moment to call my dad and with the time change, hopefully I would catch him at home. I had it all planned.

But I never made the call. I never picked up the kids.

After loading the back of the car with groceries, I climbed up into the driver's seat and arranged my purse on the center console. When I turned to close the door, there was a man standing next to me. In a matter of seconds, he pushed his way into the car and locked the doors. He shoved something sharp against my side.

Many have nightmares: Mine came true. I was forced into the furthest back seat of the Suburban with no windows or doors to open for escape. I tried my hardest to defend myself, but after being severely beaten and stabbed, my blood splattering across the seat before my eyes, I realized that if I did not comply, I would no doubt be killed right there, in broad daylight, in the parking lot of Ralph's Grocery Store.

The man raped me while repeatedly punching me in the face and screaming at me. When he had finished, he announced that we would be going for a drive. I knew he intended to kill me. The enormity of the SUV with its tinted windows had made for the perfect prison until this point, but finally opportunity came my way. There was no way for him to drive and keep me in the back seat at the same time. It was 3:30 on a sunny afternoon in wealthy Brentwood, California. The parking lot was far from empty, so he decided he had better get out of there fast.

He chose to leave me in the back, commanding me to stay put. As soon as he got to the front, I leapt into the center seat and desperately tried to get out of the car. At that point I was so hysterical that I couldn't even figure out how the door locks worked. I pressed every button on the door in despair, and as though a beacon was suddenly showing the way, the window began opening just as the car began to back out of the parking spot. I barely remember jumping out, but somehow I squeezed through the opening, and as he tore out of the parking lot, I ran for my life into the supermarket.

The police were called immediately, and an ambulance took me to the Santa Monica Rape Treatment Center. Fortunately, the beast left his DNA behind and although it has yet to match any other in the databanks, I have hope he will someday be found so no other woman will have to endure his torture and terrorizing.

My life changed that day. The life I'd lived before getting into the car was over. The 'Me' I'd known my whole life was obliterated. Physically: a mess. Emotionally: destroyed. But I had survived, and survivors have that rare opportunity to start over. I used to think the person I'd once been was dead and that with her died her independence and self-reliance. It's true, that woman was gone, but I've come to discover that those thirty minutes in violent captivity were in fact what led to my rebirth. I wasn't dead; I was very much alive. But I wasn't me anymore.

One day I caught a glimmer of the hope that would be the source of my healing. I was taking my first shower since I'd left the hospital. I'd been too afraid and in far too much pain to attempt before. Now it had been a couple days, but I had been putting it off because the shower at the Rape Treatment Center had been so awful: I could barely stand up; my hair was falling out in clumps, and it was so matted there was no way to wash it. A nurse had to cut a chunk of it out. This was my last shower memory, and I was afraid to wash away more of myself. As if bathing might cause me to lose the last part of my identity I was grasping onto. The funk I lived in those first couple of days comforted me somehow. Or maybe just distracted me. I wasn't really living, just going through the motions. Ice on the face, ice off the face … Look at the bruises; stare at my unrecognizable face in the mirror. I replayed the attack uncontrollably in my head like a skipping DVD. (I always said "attack," like it was less scary, more general than the "R word" …)

I wanted out of the funk I guess, because I finally took a shower. What happened in the shower changed my life. The cleansing of the water opened up something in my consciousness. I'd had visions before that guided me to do things in my life, but this was a vision that connected every vision I'd ever had together, as if everything in my life had been leading up to this one moment.

Standing there with the water running over me, something besides two days of dirt was washed away: sadness, anger, guilt, confusion, helplessness, loss of control, terror, self-pity … everything, for one brief moment. I came to an understanding that was instantaneous. Clarity washed over me, and I suddenly understood why I'd had this horrific experience: why I'd been chosen to be the victim of such brutal violence. I remember the moment as if I were watching a movie of the future of my life. The movie seemed to play on fast forward, so I don't recall the specifics, but as they replay as reality in my life, I remember them from that moment in the shower.

I got out of the shower a different woman. I immediately told my boyfriend that I realized I'd been raped and assaulted in order to do what I needed to do with my life. I told him that I would someday write and perform my story, and I'd be able to relate to other women's similar experiences around the world. My story of being "victimized" would one day empower me to help others come forward to share their experiences. A new collective voice among women and all of humanity could be created where until now there had been far too much silence. I envisioned creating an organization to bring together survivors to express their stories and the feelings experienced through the healing process. In empowering women to rid them-selves of the shame and secrecy that surrounds rape, we would create a new population of women strengthened by our experience instead of victimized. In uniting, using all forms of creative expression, we would together address the notion of violence and begin to tackle the great feat of ending it.

These moments of clarity brought me joy and even excitement. I had always felt like I had a mission in life, but so many pieces of the puzzle were missing. Then after a trauma like I had never imagined, this vision came, and suddenly my whole life made sense. Everything fit into place, even if just for a moment. I wish I could say that my healing progressed steadily from there, but the clarity soon clouded.

It has now been two years since that life-changing event, and the healing has come in waves. It's a strange thing to feel your identity splinter and have to work madly to keep yourself together. Some days I run errands without a care in the world, and other days leave me crying in a parking lot because someone walked too close to my car. It's a challenge, but I have seen the potential of my own courage, and I look forward to a day when I realize I have moved on, and all that lingers from this experience is the strength it has brought me. I tap into that strength to draw from this terrible event the power to manifest my vision from that day in the shower. I have struggled, I have cried, I have screamed in frustration and anger, but each day I move closer to creating the reality of my vision. I have now founded *Survivors & Artists for Abolishing Violence* (SAAV), an organization dedicated to developing a collective community voice using creative expression to empower survivors to share their stories and spread awareness on the issue of violence.

I am startled but ecstatic as I become more and more aware of the synchronicities that have led me to today. I have been an actor since I was a young girl and also spent years working as an events producer. I have poured countless passionate hours into political and social activism and done all sorts of public speaking. All of these experiences created a solid foundation for my new career as founder and executive director of SAAV. I look forward to producing events and performances as tools to spreading awareness of violence against women and against humanity. For years, I have dreamt of being part of a movement that unites artists with the belief that through creativity, we connect to our higher purpose.

After my horrific experience my life now has a purpose greater than before. Somehow the most terrifying, horribly negative experience of my life has become a gift, teaching me positivity and compassion. This potential lies within each of us: not just to turn negative into positive, but to trust that we are always being drawn to our calling. We all have the power to change, and we certainly don't have to experience tragedy to do it. As a survivor, I feel a responsibility to follow a calling of service. I have experienced something that I must use to help others or else I remain a victim. I am not a victim. I'm a survivor. Being raped did not destroy me. Before it happened I might have thought it could, but I have somehow gained power from the experience. We all have access to this power. We just have to figure out what to do with it.

~ *Jane Piper*

My Birth Day

Ward's Island at night was like being in another time and place miles away from the skyscrapers of Toronto that I could see directly across the harbor. Chugging through the dark water, the outline of white lights shaping the oval ferryboat seemed to glitter in joy, until the moment was interrupted by the loud blast of the horn announcing its arrival at the Toronto island port. The steel bridge dropped onto the dock, and I was greeted by Lazarus, one of the crewmembers I had befriended during the many tours back and forth to the artist retreat at Gibraltar Point where I had spent the last few months writing my second book. It was too late for the tourists to be returning to the city, so I was the only person boarding at that time. Once on the ferry I immediately went up the stairs to the upper deck and made my way to the bow of the boat where I sat on a bench seat that was positioned perfectly for a view of the city. I couldn't wait to call my mum.

As soon as the ferry pulled away, I dialed her number on my cell phone. "Huh … hello." She answered in a half-finished breath that started before the receiver reached her mouth.

"Mum, it's Susan." I spoke clearly so she could hear me. "Is everything all right?" She yelled back, asking, "Where are you this time?"

I was always calling her from different places in the world, and when I told her I was on the ferry returning to the city, she became concerned again. "It's dark out now. Are you alone?" she said.

"Yes." I answered quickly, anxious to ask her the question that was on my mind. "I'm fine, really, Mum. I need to ask you something. Can you tell me everything you remember around the story about how I got my name?"

"Oh, Susan. I've told you that story so many times, why do you want to hear it again?" I tried to be patient with her. "Mum, with seven children you know how you are always getting our stories mixed up. This is the only one about me that you can recall clearly. Please, tell me the story again. It's important to me." She began to speak, but the engine noise drowned out her soft voice, making it sound distant, almost dreamlike. I listened carefully to the familiar story that had given me a sense of hope for my entire life. I had been told this story so often that I could recite the events of that day by memory. If there were parts of the story that my parents couldn't recall, then I took the liberty of filling in the details using my imagination. While she talked I imagined the story as I had seen it in my mind.

It was March 8th and my mum was only 23 years old. She was pregnant with her second baby, and she hoped it would be a boy. Contractions had started that afternoon, and by early evening she couldn't bear the pain. Unable to reach my dad, she called his best friend Hughie to take her to the hospital. Hughie was a kind-hearted man who seemed larger than life, and he agreed to come right away. He arrived in his big car ready to save the day. My mum was in a lot of pain, and she was frightened because she didn't know what to expect this time. She laid down on the back seat of the car and prayed. I can only imagine how alone she must have felt, like she was a stranger in her own body.

There was a freak snowstorm that night delaying traffic everywhere, so it took a long time for Hughie to get to the hospital even though he drove fast. When he pulled up to the emergency entrance at St. Michael's Hospital in Toronto, my mum was relieved that they had arrived safely. He jumped out and quickly opened the back door for her. I could picture my mum biting her lower lip with her front teeth as she struggled to get out of the car. The automatic doors of the hospital banged loudly as they opened, releasing a strong antiseptic smell into the cold night air. The announcements over the speaker system were in a coded language that made no sense to her at all. She looked around and noticed people lingering in the waiting room, as if something were about to happen. She saw a young child who was whimpering in pain. There was a drunken man whose bloody face moved stiffly as he babbled nonsense to himself. An elderly woman rocked back and forth holding her arm. Then the Mother Superior entered the area, calling out orders to the staff, and my mum was told to go over to a glass window and register. Hughie left her alone in the lineup of patients while he went back outside to park the car.

While standing in the line she noticed a young nurse approaching from the end of a long corridor. She appeared to be gliding through all the commotion with ease and grace. Her starched white hat sat high on her head, and she smiled at everyone she passed. When she saw my mum, she recognized the fear in her eyes, and she came over to her. Speaking with compassion in her voice, she told my mum what she could expect and assured her that everything would be fine. At the same time, the kind nurse gently massaged her pregnant belly with both hands. Her nurturing words to my mum were spoken with a keen sense of maternal patience. For the first time since arriving at the hospital, she felt calm. Then the nurse was called to an emergency and had to leave.

Almost right away my dad arrived, and she told him about the kindness of this special nurse. They both watched her move from one patient to the next. She seemed driven by a sense of divine purpose and filled with a loving spirit. Her slender body moved gracefully through the clinical space. My dad got her attention, and when she came over, he introduced himself. "Hi, I'm Bill Regan, and this is my wife June. I want to personally thank you for taking extra care of her." The nurse smiled and bowed her head slightly in acknowledgement. Then she announced with delight that her name was Susan Regan. They tried to determine if the families were somehow related, but the only common element was that both families were originally from County Cork, Ireland. My dad offered to buy her a coffee, but she had to get back to work. Before leaving she assured them they would have a very special baby who would grow up to contribute something great to the world.

The triage nurse called my mum's name and took her to the delivery room. Hughie came back and proudly joined my dad in the father's waiting room. Several hours later I was born, a healthy baby girl with a loud voice. My parents had already decided that if I was a boy my name would be Michael, but they hadn't chosen a name for a girl. My mum was really impressed by the nurse, and she thought that if I grew up to become like her, then maybe I *would* be a great contribution to the universe. My mum's voice got louder. "And so we decided to name you Susan Regan." She spoke proudly. We named you after the special nurse with the hope that one day you would be like her."

I wanted to be completely certain of the details of the story, so I asked her again. "Mum, are you sure the nurse's name was Susan Regan?" She replied confidently, "Oh yes, I'm sure because I remember your dad having a conversation with her about where our families came from in Ireland. Why are you asking all these questions about your name?"

It was time for me to tell her about the incredible day I had experienced. Earlier, I had attended a meeting that was held at St. Andrew's Church on the Toronto Islands with a group of people who had a common interest in healing. At the beginning of the meeting, we sat in a circle and passed a talking stick around, giving each person the chance to speak. Some people shared their dreams, some told stories, and others spoke about their lives.

On the phone, I tried to explain this experience to my mum in a way that she would understand. I told her about a quiet-spoken, attractive woman across from me, who sat very still as she listened to my story. When it was her turn to speak, she announced her name was Susan. She spoke with such conviction, I could almost feel the energy and passion coming though her voice.

"Mum, she told us she had been a nurse when she was young. Then she married, changed her name, and had five children. After the birth of her fourth baby she struggled through an emotional dark period where she was briefly hospitalized and was then forced to recover from prescribed drugs. She healed by using artistic expression, and she became an accomplished artist inspiring others through her paintings. Mum, are you there?" I asked.

"Yes, yes. I am listening. What else did she say?"

"At the end of the meeting, she came over to me because she said she felt a strong connection with me. I mentioned to her that I was from a big family, and her story made me think a lot about what you had to endure. Then I asked her if any of her children were born at St. Michael's Hospital in Toronto. She told me she was a nurse in the emergency ward at St. Michael's hospital in Toronto in the late1950s. Can you believe that?" There was no response.

"I asked her what her maiden name was, and she said it was Susan Regan." There was a long silent pause.

"I told her that as a young child I would often ask you to tell me the story about how I got my name. For as long as I can remember, I have dreamed about meeting the woman whom I was named after. In some way, over time, she had become my mentor." Thinking about her often made me wonder what it would be like to be adopted without ever knowing your biological parents.

"Mum, I told her that my name was also Susan Regan. For a

moment, we just stood there looking at each other. Then I said that I believed she was the person I was named after." There she was right in front of me, and even more special than I could have imagined. I couldn't explain to my mum what happened next because she wouldn't understand what I was talking about. I began to feel a physical reaction to her presence. It was as though every cell in my body was vibrating at a higher frequency. I felt like I was looking into a mirror of myself.

I continued, "We hugged, cried with joy, and then laughed out loud at the sheer coincidence of our meeting."

There was silence on the phone. "Mum, are you there?" I called out.

"Yes, Susan." She spoke quietly. Her voice was trembling. I knew that she would be moved by this story.

"You would love her. She's a caring, beautiful soul and someone I truly adore. She said she would like to meet you sometime." There was silence again. I'm sure that she never imagined I would ever meet this woman. "Mum, thank you for giving me her name and for believing that I could contribute something great to the world."

With a loud thump, the ferry jerked as it hit the tire bumpers along the docks. "I'm in Toronto now, and I have to go. I'll call you tomorrow, and we can talk more about this. OK?" There was no answer. "Bye for now, Mum." I waited to hear something from her before hanging up the phone. With a deep sigh she whispered good-bye to me. Then Lazarus called out to warn me I had to get off right away because the ferry was leaving for Hanlan's Point.

I let the phone fall away from my ear, but just as I was about to press the "End" button, I heard her voice call out to me. "I love you, Susan." Lifting the phone to my ear again, I spoke the words we rarely exchanged to each other.

"Mum, I love you too." It was too late. She had already hung up the phone, and the connection was lost. I rushed down the stairs and thanked Lazarus as I passed him. Once on the mainland, I paused to acknowledge how grateful I was to have met Susan Regan on my birthday. That day had ended, but a new journey had begun.

~ Sue Kenney

Worthy As I Am

Challenges are gifts that force us to search
for a new center of gravity.
Don't fight them. Just find a different way to stand.
— Oprah Winfrey

I sat there facing my dad, stunned at his announcement that he was selling the company. My last several years had been dedicated to supporting the home-building company in which my brothers and I were employed. My day had earned his retirement, but the news he broke next caused me to reel on my seat!

Many years before, my parents had separated when I turned fifteen. After many years of abuse, my mom finally made the very challenging decision to leave. She had been a housewife for years, so living alone in the city was scary and expensive. She barely made enough money to support herself, let alone her four children, so my two younger brothers, my sister, and I stayed with my dad. My mom was heartbroken at having to leave all of us behind.

My sister and I both acted out our grief differently, she acting tough and hiding her feelings, while I yearned even more for the love and attention I so craved. Being the oldest, I stepped into the "Mommy role," so while other kids my age hung out with friends, I did loads of laundry and cleaned the house.

My dad was very strict and sometimes terribly demanding, both in his business and with his family. He expected everyone around him to live up to his high standards. As a normal teenager would, I rebelled. And when the arguing just became too intense, I made the decision to leave immediately after graduation.

At the age of eighteen, I moved to the city with aspirations of fulfilling a lifelong dream of becoming a police officer. When my application was turned down, I was crushed and was forced to look for an alternative career path. During that time, I fell in love with my husband to be and soon became pregnant. The birth of my beautiful little girl healed my heart and helped me to overcome the loss I'd felt at not landing the job with the police force. We were married and went on to have another baby, this time a boy.

As my children grew, I became increasingly anxious to move my family back to the country, where I had grown up. My husband was hesitant, but with my coaxing he soon agreed it would be a better place to raise our two children. When my dad heard we were moving back to the area, he began planting seeds of me someday working with him in his company. The timing was perfect. I needed to get out into the workforce and make some money. This would also be an opportunity for me to begin a new career along with proving to my dad that I could be a great asset to his company. There I was again, unconsciously looking for that acceptance from my dad and that proof of my worthiness.

Dad owned a custom home company that he'd built up over ten years. He'd bought out two other owners to form the family company he'd dreamed of. My brother worked in the factory, my sister in our other model home in Ottawa, and my half brother and my youngest brother worked with us as well. This truly was a family company, or at least so I thought.

Working for my dad wasn't easy. He was a perfectionist, and he demanded that perfectionism of those around him. He expected long hours and total commitment. Hard work and profits were top priorities for him.

I was always striving to impress him, working diligently selling and then managing the sales office for over seven years. Many times I worked during family occasions and weekends. I was totally committed to the business and my work, maybe too much. The years passed by so quickly. I didn't realize how much I was driven by my need for acceptance.

One day my dad came into my office. My insecurities immediately arose—had I done something wrong? Then my dad broke the startling news: he'd decided to retire and sell the company. I felt slightly surprised, although my dad had worked very hard all his life and deserved time off to enjoy his rewards. I felt excited too, because after all, this was a family company, and this would be a great opportunity for me to be more involved financially.

The next few seconds seemed like an eternity, moving in slow motion as he went on to say he was selling the company to my younger brother and two other male managers who were not family. I was in a deep state of shock and disbelief.

This could not be true … What about me? My husband and I were divorcing at the time, so it was a very hard time emotionally already.

I recall saying to my dad, "You're kidding, right? This is a family company! Why am I not being included?"

My dad's comment was "You can't have four partners. You have to have only have three." He was very calm, as if he had already rehearsed this in his mind. This made no sense to me. Two, three and four people own companies all the time! This was an excuse, not a reason, and a weak one at that.

I had worked so hard, I had committed myself to this company, and I was dedicated. I felt like someone had just punched me in the stomach, and all the life went out of me. I begged my dad to include me, but he'd made up his mind.

Several times on the way home I thought of driving straight into a ditch. I felt worthless, not worthy of love or success. The illusion in which I'd invested so much time and love had been torn apart. But as I thought of my children, I knew I could never leave them alone. I had no way of knowing then that God was trying to give me a gift.

I struggled for months, every day putting on a happy face. After all, I ran a sales office, and I was responsible to carry on as if nothing had happened. But in spite of my brave face, everything changed. The owners now made sure to put me in my place at every opportunity. I was just an employee now, not an intricate part of the company, not an involved part of the team.

This change began to eat away at me. I turned my anger toward my dad. I felt he had been very selfish. By now he'd bought a boat and sailed down to the Bahamas. His life was sweet. My brother's life changed significantly too; once the factory manager, he was now an owner of a multi-million dollar company. All of this was too hard to swallow. I became bitter and angry, finding comfort in self-pity. I wallowed in it, carrying anger on my shoulders for years, until finally I was struck with a serious illness that affected my liver. I became yellow with jaundice.

In my deepest low, nothing else mattered but my health. All this pettiness, all this anger I had been carrying around meant nothing. I knew God was asking me to make a decision: I could poison myself with anger, or find a way to forgive and love again.

I recall lying in bed, thinking, "Why me? I am a good person. I work hard. I am a good mom." Then I realized this was a lesson for me. This illness was God telling me to slow down, to listen to myself, so that I could delve deeper into the meaning of this lesson. Then I got it!

The acceptance I needed wasn't from my dad, my brother, or my ex-husband. It was from myself! With this new awareness I was finally able to forgive my father. I felt the weight of years of bitterness and anger lifting from my life.

As I turned a corner in my healing, I met a wonderful man who saw me for who I really was: a worthy, beautiful, dynamic woman. With new love came new opportunities and a whole new beginning. We built a new home, I got a new job, and we started planning our future together.

I was taking baby steps to freedom while deep inside I could feel my self-esteem building. I began to think, 'Maybe I could be happy again?'

Now I needed to focus on getting better and moving forward in my life. I needed to redirect my focus to all of the great things in my life: my children, my family, my friends, my new love, but first and foremost, my health. Step by step I worked on this and eventually recovered fully.

A couple of years later, another company, a competitor of my previous family business, approached me with an offer. They were doing a province-wide recruitment of proven sales people in the industry. They wanted me. Doubt entered my mind. Could they really want me? Could I leave the one product I had known now for years? Was I prepared to try something new? What if I failed?

By now I knew that I was capable of doing great things. I could always pick myself up and try something else. At the same time, I decided to go back to school to get my diploma in business. I knew it would be tough, working full time and going to school, but I was determined. The five years until graduation passed by so quickly! I could feel my self-esteem flooding in.

One day, a revelation struck me. I was my own person! I was a good person! And most importantly, I was a worthy person! I'd finally grown up.

Letting go of my insecurities has allowed space for new opportunities. Along with my sales career, I am co-hosting a television show called "Daytime" on Rogers Television and assisting my husband in his business, touring clients overseas. Over the last few years my relationship with my father has changed significantly. Now when we talk, I feel equal to him, and I sense a newfound respect coming from him. After years of always looking for acceptance, I realize I never really needed it. I already had it within myself.

Today the fear of failing has left me. I have this incredible feeling inside me that if I plan for the best, amazing things can happen.

~ *Darlene Christianson*

Perfect Casting

The love of God is in the very smallest things,
the most private experiences of your life.
— Harold Klemp, What is Spiritual Freedom?

At first it seemed just like the multitude of other audition calls from my agent. Time, place, status, shoot dates, fee, etc., until she got to the project description, and something inside me snapped to attention. This was to be an industrial shoot, a training video for the staff of our city's transit system, designed to help prevent the regular use of the subway trains to end desperate lives.

SUICIDE! That word had become a close companion in 1991 when my beleaguered mother, in another city, on another transit system, dispassionately and methodically lay down under a train. So I had a personal connection to this project, but I was still to learn how personal.

I read for the role of a mother who suspects that her daughter is contemplating suicide. I thought the audition went well, but in this highly erratic business, "Excellent!" "Perfect!" or even "That's exactly what we are looking for!" is no guarantee that you land the role. So, as I always try to do, I forgot about the job.

A couple of weeks later, my agent called to tell me that I didn't get the part I had auditioned for, but another role instead. Although this role was to be non-speaking, I would be paid the same rate as the speaking parts. I was to be 'The Jumper,' the person who jumps in front of the train. Now this was beyond personal; this was core.

An actor must get into the very essence of a character and what that person is experiencing. And although I had more or less dealt with my mother's violent and tragic demise, a part of me had vanished into another dimension where I was experiencing life as through Plexiglas.

I had several days to prepare and to create my character, a woman who would sob uncontrollably while seated on a bench at the subway station. Then in another scene, she would coolly and detachedly place her jacket, purse, and shoes on the bench and go off to end her life.

Even though I had done a lot of therapy and work around the impact of my mother's suicide, I knew I was now being invited to walk down her road. I entered into long, careful, and probing discussions with my youngest sister, who had identified what was left of my mother's body at the morgue. We focused on our mother's life, her unlived dreams, her burdens, and her pain. My sister worried about the toll of this exploration on me, knowing firsthand the searing horror this experience had irrevocably burned on our family. But I knew this was something I had to do.

I dug out my mother's suicide note. At the time of her death, it seemed like gibberish, but now it made perfect sense. I even managed to dip into the box of her letters, which I hadn't touched in fourteen years. I was starting to see life through her eyes.

On the day of the shoot, the production assistant met me at the midtown subway station. He led me through an unmarked door, down to another level. To my shock, there at the foot of the stairs was a whole other subway station.

It was identical to the one above, only filthy and dilapidated. I had not known of this station's existence, but it seems it had been constructed as an interim connection during subway line expansion.

Now abandoned, it was used for film and TV shoots. 'The Forgotten Level Below'—the symbolism erupted in my awareness!

The hair and makeup guy was someone with whom I had previously worked, and I liked him. I relaxed under his gentle touch. While he worked on me, I wondered about the 'crying scene' to come.

I had achieved the ability to cry on demand a couple of years earlier, after having to put down my dog of eighteen and a half years, Toto. Remembering that experience had fueled an acting job I did afterward. Now I wondered if I'd be able to control the tears once they started. The director wanted to do the crying scene first. The cameramen set up the shot and put me in position. In my head, I began to recite lines of the poem my mother had written in her suicide note…

'I've been working on the railroad all the live long day…'

So tired, so—so—so tired …

'I've been working on the railroad just to pass the time away…'

Suddenly I understood my mother's pain: life can seem so pointless, meaningless—for nothing … FLOODGATES OPENED!

I sat there sobbing my pain, her pain, and our pain. Sometimes life is so hard. Sometimes no matter what you do, it doesn't work. Sometimes there is no reason to go on. Sometimes there is nothing to cling to and no one to understand …

The director interrupted my heaving sobs and tumbling thoughts. "We need to make an adjustment to the camera, so if you'd like to step put of character for a few moments till we're ready again …" There it was—Divine Intervention: the reminder that the whole of life is just a play. As Shakespeare wrote in the play *As You Like It* :

All the world's a stage

And all the men and women merely players:

They have their exits and their entrances;

And one man in his time plays many parts. …

My mom was gone, but so was her pain, and much of what her

life was about. Only the love remained. The director returned. "We are ready again, so if you'd like to get back into character … "I instantly began to sob once more until he said, "Cut!" He thanked me for a job well done, and as I left the scene the cameraman said, "We all need a good cry now and then." When I'd finished my two other scenes, I felt relief and a great sense of accomplishment at working through this experience.

Above all, I realized that the love of Holy Spirit is so great that Its care of our lives, even to the smallest detail, is miraculous. Spirit had cast me precisely in the right place, time, and circumstance for me to have a profound healing, in a way that was natural and appropriate for me. It had also arranged for me to participate in a drama that would bring comfort and healing to others on a larger scale. And I got paid. How perfect is that!

~ Janine Gwendoline Smith

Healing My Heart

"I cannot teach you how to pray in words.
God listens not to your words save when He Himself
utters them through your lips. And I cannot teach you the
prayer of the seas and the forests and the mountains.
But you who are born of the mountains and the forests
and the seas can find their prayer in your heart.
And if you but listen in the stillness of the night you
shall hear them saying in silence, 'Our God, who art our
winged self, it is thy will in us that willeth. . . .' "
— Kahlil Gibran

I didn't get much encouragement growing up. My stories and poems were dismissed by my father as "sentimental trash," by my older sister as "emotionalism," and by my teachers as a "waste of time." I learned that it was safer to write in secret journals, where I recalled every event with great clarity, often bringing myself to tears.

By the time I was married and had children, I thought, *When they grow old enough, I'll take up my dream of writing.* I was willing to work for pennies, if necessary, at a small newspaper. I knew that I would work hard, driving people crazy about my writing, just to give them a reason to say, "Give her what she wants; just shut her up."

I finally had my chance in 1980, when I talked myself into a newspaper column illustrating the joys and sorrows of motherhood.

It wasn't long before I discovered that my husband had been molesting my oldest child, who was twelve years old. With the assistance of a caring police department and a compassionate friend, we ran to safety, just my little girls and me.

I left behind a budding writing career, since prudence required that no one know where we were. We fled in the middle of winter, and my only desire was to keep my daughters safe. I did what needed to be done. I found a job, got an apartment, and got divorced. I believed with all my heart that God would bring us through. My writing, once again, was confined to my journals and my thoughts.

Miraculously, into the lives of my children and I came a gentle, loving, trustworthy man, who has become the love of my life. We married six months after we met, and his adoption of my girls became final within a year. *My* children had become *our* children, and I was happier than I had ever been.

We raised our children with little money and lots of faith. We were a military family. There was seldom much of anything to go around, but we gave our daughters a life that declared to each of them, *You are special—you are loved.* The years passed. There was joy and sorrow, but we made it together. All this time, I continued to write and remember. I had no career except my family and the occasional job, where I worked too hard and was paid too little.

My health issues began to take center stage a month after my mother died. The stresses of my life and her death had placed a great burden upon my body and mind. I had a nervous breakdown at forty-two, and I fought with every nerve and fiber of my being just to recover. I would not give in! I would not surrender! It became an effort just to get out of bed, but I moved from under the covers, no matter how I felt, and I took those determined steps. When I couldn't walk, I crawled.

Overnight, it seemed, I was fifty-two years old, and my health had never been worse. Through the years I had developed fibromyalgia, asthma, arthritis, a heart arrhythmia, and diabetes. Emotionally, I had never been able to let go of my past. The memories haunted me every day. I was on anti-depressants, and I was taking a plethora of pills. I grasped at every "think positive" cure going around. My church group anointed and prayed over me. Television preachers promised that God would heal my ailments, if I had enough faith and would send them a nice donation. But my asthma got worse, and so did my depression.

That's when I began to understand that anyone's "ten-step plan" was *not* going to rescue me. So I turned to God and only Him. I spent hours, days, weeks, months imploring God to either heal me or tell me why I wouldn't heal. It took a year and a half for me to finally be ready for His answer.

One day I began to hear a voice—a voice that had always been there, speaking to me in a soft whisper. A voice that told me, "I love you more than you know." As I knelt there, my mind finally silent and waiting, I heard God's voice, as clear in my heart as the call of a bird to my ear.

"Jaye," said the voice. "What do you want?"

"To be healed, Lord. To be healed."

"Are you ready?"

"Yes, Lord, please heal my body! Take away my asthma! Take away my suffering!" I pleaded.

"Jaye, I will give you healing, but you must choose what I will heal—your asthma or that aching heart that is tearing you apart." Wow! I didn't like that choice! Couldn't He do both? I mean, this was God, after all! I knelt there for what seemed like days, just thinking. What would be my choice? Suddenly I knew. My depression had been like a heavy, black shroud that had eclipsed my life and banished my joy for as long as I could remember. It was then that I knew the answer.

"Lord, if I can have only one healing, please heal my depression!"

I meant every word. In some eternity between heaven and earth, I felt God smile.

God's answer came swiftly. "Medical science will heal your asthma, but I will transform your heart!" Every ounce of my being surrendered. I could feel God's gentle withdrawal, but His love remained within me. No matter what the world threw at me, I knew that God loved me. My physical health did not improve overnight, but my heart was transformed forever. Since then, there has grown between God and me a warm, steady friendship.

Sure enough, medical science began to pour out new drugs to control asthma, and remarkably, new drugs were also introduced to control all my other aches and pains. With every effort that I made to let go of my self-pity, God blessed my life a thousand-fold. Growing within my soul was a sacred intimacy, and that was where I began to understand God's gift of grace for the very first time.

I began to write soon after. My words began to explode onto my computer screen and in time across the internet. I began to get published as I communicated God's blessings in my life. In trusting God to guide each word and each step, I have found a rewarding writing career. Communicating about God's truth, grace, and love in my life has also given me precious friendships throughout the world. Out of His grace I have been given a new sense of perspective, seeing beyond the ashes of my broken dreams, and finding beauty and hope within.

It is true that many of my stories have won awards, and they have found their way into books of inspiration and encouragement. This is wonderful, but it's not why I write. I write because I now understand that my greatest prison was the one that I carried within myself. And the greatest freedom I have ever known was that moment of surrender to God, when I chose His healing within my heart.

~ *Jaye Lewis*

Reaching Into Myself

We must be willing to get rid of the life we've planned,
so as to have the life that is waiting for us.
— Joseph Campbell

My conscious journey began in 1998 with one swollen joint on one finger on one hand. I could recall nothing that I might have done to injure my finger. Time and medication did nothing to reduce the swelling.

After many exploratory questions and tests, I was told I had an autoimmune disease, likely lupus. Symptoms I hadn't thought too much of, with the exception of the swollen finger, were identified as signs that pointed to my immune response gone wrong, to the likely presence of a disease for which no cure is known.

I was twenty-six years old when this news dropped like a dead weight into my life. At the time, I was working in telecommunications, a career path I'd reluctantly stumbled onto when the job market seemed to provide little choice. My fine arts degree, though very valuable education, had not inspired any particular direction. I took a job answering customer calls and later accepted a promotion in a customer service support role.

I worked with a great team of people and was gaining tremendous experience. There were even days when I could see myself climbing the corporate ladder, though most often there was a nagging, barely conscious sense that this was not my life's work.

My company turned out to be an incredibly supportive place to be as my health became compromised. One swollen joint progressed to inflammation in 70 percent of the joints in my body, with particular intensity in my hands. When other symptoms escalated and new ones appeared, I was given the option to take a leave of absence from my job. My supervisor and teammates supported me by staying in touch and letting me know how much they cared. This was some of the best medicine I received.

My leave from work began as a time to slow down. The greatest gift the first specialist gave me lay in her explanation of autoimmune disease. She told me that essentially it is the self not recognizing the self. These words penetrated deep within me to a place where I understood that this was not just about my physical body. How far away from myself had I traveled to be at this place? My leave from work became a time to stop altogether and to gather what I needed to start again.

I began a dialogue with my whole self—as fragmented, confused and disconnected as I felt. It became my work to discover how to recognize myself. I was introduced to health care professionals who encouraged me to devote my energy to becoming well. I began to examine my life, not just my body, for all the places that felt healthy and unhealthy. My recovery included the end to some relationships and the beginning of others. And I began cultivating the most important relationship of all, the one with myself.

With the support of medical doctors who monitored my health, the intervention of various complementary therapies and counseling, lifestyle changes, and the help of family and friends, I began to experience greater wellness. I regained more ease in the use of my hands and movement of my body. My emotions and spirit began to find their voices, and my mind found some peace.

I went back to my job in telecommunications for a while before moving on to develop partnerships for a nonprofit organization. Here, too, I was met with wonderful teammates and great support for what this next stretch of my life would hold.

But that world brought with it a disregard for my new gift of wellness. I felt so good that I began celebrating in ways that compromised my health. Then I discovered my body had become a gauge for the state of my health on all levels. It screamed on the outside when something on the inside was not in balance. At the same time, it was showing me what I was to do with my career path.

Eventually, the specialist following my case told me to keep doing what I was doing to be healthy and that I didn't need him anymore. Symptoms of the autoimmune disease were gone.

Friends and acquaintances had begun to ask what I was doing to be well. I became interested in career options within the healing arts, and so I tested the waters with a few courses.

I entered into a full-time training program in Polarity Therapy, and it moved me in ways I had not thought I could move. It challenged me to go to places within myself that I hadn't known existed. The work got grounded in me, through the hands-on experiences of touching and being touched in powerful, profoundly healing ways. It took me deeper into consciousness, to a presence with myself I had only previously begun to explore.

I went on to study cranial sacral therapy, and later, relaxation massage. My first bodywork teacher described the healing arts as an infinite field best served by continually deepening and expanding the well from which you draw. By doing so, my life continues to grow in infinite ways.

Today, much of the bodywork I do is with people in long-term care. Most are elderly, with chronic pain and degenerative diseases. Some are younger, in need of constant care for the pain and disease that has altered the course of their lives. The care I offer them doesn't take all the pain away or cure disease. In many cases it simply provides some temporary relief and a hand to hold. An eighty-year-old woman I work with recently asked if I have my hands insured. She tells me they are healing hands. A sixty-three-year-old man said after the first session, "I feel like I've been touched by an angel."

The divine irony is that the work I do now flows primarily through my hands. It was not that long ago that to hold a pen to write caused me pain. Today, the use of my hands to reach out to others is a gift that moves me to tears. And it is made possible only by continually reaching into myself.

~ *Karen Haffey*

4

The lift of Higher Vision

"There is no need to run outside for better seeing...

rather abide at the center of your being;

for the more you leave it, the less you learn.

Search your heart and see...

the way to do is to be."

— Lao Tzu (6th century B.C.)

Marching Orders

I began teaching the creativity workshops in New York. I taught them because I was *told* to teach them. One minute I was walking in the West Village on a cobblestone street with a beautiful afternoon light. The next minute I suddenly knew that I should begin teaching people, groups of people, how to unblock. Maybe it was a wish exhaled on somebody else's walk. Certainly Greenwich Village must contain a greater density of artists—blocked and otherwise—than nearly anyplace else in America.

"I need to unblock," someone may have breathed out.

"I know how to do it," I may have responded, picking up my cue. My life has always included strong internal directives.

Marching orders, I call them.

In any case, I suddenly knew that I did know how to unblock people and that I was meant to do so, starting then and there with the lesson I myself had learned.

Where did the lesson come from?

In 1978, in January, I stopped drinking. I had never thought drinking made me a writer, but now I suddenly thought not drinking might make me stop. In my mind, drinking and writing went together like, well, scotch and soda. For me the trick was always getting past the fear and onto the page. I was playing beat the clock—trying to write before the booze closed in like fog and my window of creativity was blocked again.

By the time I was thirty and abruptly sober, I had an office on the

Paramount lot and had made a whole career out of that kind of creativity. Creative in spasms. Creative as an act of will and ego. Creative on behalf of others. Creative, yes, but in spurts, like blood from a severed carotid artery. A decade of writing and all I knew was how to make these headlong dashes and hurl myself, against all odds, at the wall of whatever I was writing. If creativity was spiritual in any sense, it was only in its resemblance to a crucifixion. I fell upon the thorns of prose. I bled.

If I could have continued writing the old, painful way, I would certainly still be doing it. The week I got sober, I had two national magazine pieces out, a newly minted feature script, and an alcohol problem I could not handle any longer.

I told myself that if sobriety meant no creativity, I did not want to be sober. Yet I recognized that drinking would kill me *and* the creativity. I needed to learn to write sober—or else give up writing entirely. Necessity, not virtue, was the beginning of my spirituality. I was forced to find a new creative path. And that is where my lesson began.

I learned to turn my creativity over to the only god I could believe in, the god of creativity, the life force Dylan Thomas called "the force that through the green fuse drives the flower." I learned to just show up at the page and write down what I heard. Writing became more like eavesdropping and less like inventing a nuclear bomb. It wasn't so tricky, and it didn't blow up on me anymore. I didn't have to be in the mood. I didn't have to take my emotional temperature to see if inspiration was pending. I simply wrote. No negations. Good, bad? None of my business. I wasn't doing it. By resigning as the self-conscious author, I wrote freely.

In retrospect, I am astounded I could let go of the drama of being a suffering artist. Nothing dies harder than a bad idea. And few ideas are worse that the ones we have about art. We can charge so many things off to our suffering-artist identity: drunkenness, promiscuity, fiscal problems, a certain ruthlessness or self-destructiveness in matters of the heart. We all know how broke-crazy-promiscuous-unreliable artists are. And if they don't have to be, then what's my excuse?

The ideas I could be sane, sober, and creative terrified me, implying as it did the possibility of personal accountability. "You mean if I have these gifts, I'm supposed to use them?" Yes.

Providentially, I was sent another blocked writer to work with—and on—at this time. I began to teach him what I was learning. (Get of the way. Let *it* work through you. Accumulate pages, not judgments.) He, too, began to unblock. Now there were two of us. Soon I had another "victim," this one a painter. The tools worked for the visual artists, too.

This was very exciting to me. In my grander moments, I imagined I was turning into a creative cartographer, mapping a way out of confusion for myself and for whoever wanted to follow. I never planned to become a teacher. I was only angry I'd never had a teacher myself. Why did I learn what I learned the way I learned it: all by trial and error, all by walking into walls? We artists should be more teachable, I thought. Shortcuts and hazards of the trail could be flagged.

These were the thoughts that eddied with me as I took my afternoon walks—enjoying the lights off the Hudson, plotting what I would write next. Enter the marching orders: I was to teach.

Within a week, I was offered a teaching position and space at the New York Feminist Art Institute—which I had never heard of. My first class—blocked painters, novelists, poets, and filmmakers—assembled itself. I began teaching them the lessons that are now in the book *The Artist's Way,* which became a best selling book. Since that class there have been many others, and many more lessons as well.

The Artist's Way began as informal class notes. As word of mouth spread, I began mailing out packets of materials. Next the creation spirituality network got word of the work, and people wrote from Dubuque, British Columbia, Indiana. Students materialized all over the globe. "I am in Switzerland with the state department. Please send me…." So I did.

Many times I've heard words to the effect: "Before I took your class, I was completely separate from my creativity."

I doubt that I can convey to you the feeling of the miraculous that I experience as a teacher, witnessing the before and after in the lives of students. The same charged spiritual atmosphere that fills a great work of art can fill a creativity class. In a sense, when we are creative beings, our lives become a work of art.

~ *Julia Cameron*

A Matter of Perspective

*To offer no resistance to life is to be in a state of grace,
ease, and lightness — Eckhart Tolle*

In the dream I am working on a very large oil painting. This is strange, as oil is not my chosen medium. I usually paint in gouache and aquarelle. I am fervently working up close on a pair of hands. Over and over again I try to get it right, but each time my endeavor is less than satisfactory. Fastidiously, I rub off the paint, erasing and then trying again to reach some kind of perfection. The strategically placed strokes and carefully blended colors are wiped away into oblivion with a turpentine-soaked rag. My frustration mounts, and each time my effort increases.

Suddenly, I feel the gentle pressure of a hand on my shoulder. The unknown presence invites me to step back, further and further still. I turn to look at the painting, and my jaw drops in shock. There before me, the hands have receded into an enormous Work of Art, resplendent in its total beauty.

In amazement, I realize that I had been too close, and therefore I was unable to see the whole picture, which I now realize is perfect.

I awaken filled with gratitude at this incredible "Life Lesson," given vividly with so much love, patience, and meaning. It's all in how we look and from where we look—a matter of perspective.

~ Janine Gwendoline Smith

The Day I Died

Each of us has an inner dream that we can unfold if we will
just have the courage to admit what it is. And the faith to
trust our own admission.

— Julia Cameron

At the age of two, on a miserable hot day in August, I drowned.

I remember the day vividly. Three families' worth of sticky, sweaty
children tumbled out of the car and scampered in bare feet down the
scalding hot, sandy bank to the clean, cool Connecticut River below.
I heard my mother tell my brother and sister to keep an eye on me
while she sat with her friends. I watched my brother and sister take
their places in line under the Smith Covered Bridge. One by one, the
laughing kids took turns swinging from it, splashing into the water,
and rising back up out of it. I wanted to be a big kid, but I didn't
know how to swim. I knew the rules: Don't go in the water up over
my knees, and don't go near the drop-off.

I tried to catch minnows in my bucket, but even the minnows
didn't want to play with me. I kicked my legs and walked around on
the sandy bottom on my hands. A mean little boy came out of the
water and made fun of me: "You're not really swimming." I was
embarrassed. I decided to see if I could swim. I dunked my whole
head under the water and opened my eyes. I lifted my arms and
moved them like water wings. I began to fall. I kicked and swiveled in

search of the surface. I was sinking to the bottom! I looked up and saw the sun shining through the water. My chest hurt. Then pop! There was no time left.

No one heard my silent screaming; no one heard my telepathic cry for help. I saw a fairy, like the one in the Walt Disney movies on TV Sunday nights. Tinkerbell waved her wand, and I saw my body floating in the water, my hair moving in the river currents. My body was motionless. I began to see a movie of my life playing backwards. At the end of my movie, I saw a man with long brown hair and a white robe floating towards me. He wasn't in the water. He was in the air. His robe billowed gently; his hair flowed softly around his head. I asked him why the movie had stopped. I noticed I could see his hands and wrists, but couldn't see his feet. I asked, "Who are you, and where are your feet?"

He smiled. The next moment I was sitting on a stone bench under olive trees in the Garden of Gethsemane. He told me that if I could survive the first part of my life, which would be a very, very hard thing to accomplish, that I would move to the place where movies are made.

He said that I would tell what was taken out of the Bible. He said Mary Magdalene was my soul mother and that he was my soul father. He told me they said bad things about my mother, the Magdalene, but that they weren't true. He told me not to be frightened, to be like her. We were from the tribe of Benjamin, and that was a good thing. He said they took the word reincarnation out of the Bible, but I would remember my past lives. He said when I was old enough that I would teach Truth—the truth about life.

The next thing I remember is a man in a red bathing suit swimming towards me. I was back in my body. I felt the man grasp my arm and lift me to him. He swam for a little while with me under his arm. Then he handed me to my mother. She didn't want to hear anything about what Jesus had told me.

When I became a mother myself, I had another near-death experience. Over a four-year time span, from age 19 to 23, I had a recurring precognitive dream that I was to give birth to twins, and one would die. When an ultrasound revealed that I was pregnant with twins, I kept hoping that the dream was just a warning that I should focus on the meticulous medical care needed to carry both babies to term.

During that pregnancy, my husband began to display appalling behavior. I spoke to many people about my concerns. From doctors to ministers and other mothers, relatives, and friends, the consensus was consistent: Ignore his behavior, and he would adjust to becoming a father. So I ignored my own intuition and endured his verbal, emotional, and mental abuse. One night he came home drunk and high on drugs. He woke me from a deep sleep. He bore all of his weight down on to me as I lay screaming in the missionary position for him to stop. Deaf to my pain, he entered me fiercely, past my swollen belly, and moved like a jackhammer breaking up cement. His actions promptly brought on premature labor.

The day after giving birth, the doctors sent me home, despite the fact that I was complaining of back and groin pain, while my babies remained in intensive care. For twelve days the girls fought to breathe while I ignored the signs of extreme pain in my own body and kept driving the long journey on back roads to and from the hospital. I pumped breast milk for them and froze it, trusting that some day they would be strong enough to drink it from a feeding tube and then, hopefully, directly from my own breasts.

Within a week, my health condition had gotten so severe that I couldn't move my legs. As I lay in bed, the memory of what had happened to me began to resurface. I was so ashamed and felt so responsible for the condition of the twins. Why hadn't I listened to my own knowing? By not listening to myself, I had put my children in harm's way. My husband cried in my arms and apologized. He and I both wanted to believe he had made a mistake.

The next day the hospital called and said if my husband and I wanted to see our daughter alive, we had better get over there right away. She was dead before we got there.

Shortly after the news of my daughter's death, I was admitted into the hospital with a 16-inch blood clot in my right leg and a 14-inch blood clot in my left leg. Tests were done that indicated that my inferior vena cava, the big blue vein in the abdomen that pumps the blood from our heart and lungs to the venous vein system in the legs, had permanently clotted and collapsed in me. If those clots moved, I would either have a stroke or die.

The doctors told my husband that I might not live through the night. My husband did not stay with me. He couldn't look me in the eye. Instead, he left me alone in the hospital.

During the night I had another near-death experience. My great-grandmother appeared and told me that it was not my time to die. She said that she had also had twins, and one had died. She said that she would take care of my daughter for me. I could see them together. Gram sternly informed me that I was needed on the earth plane to be of service to others after the twins. She told me to look in her desk in the family Bible, and I would find a prayer that she had written in her own handwriting. When my mother came to visit me the next day, I told her about my experience. I had been telling Mom my predictions and visions since I was little. She knew about my twin premonition. She confirmed that Great Grammie Farmington had had twins and one died. She had not told me before about Grammie's twins because she didn't want me to worry that this pattern ran in the family. She had known that there was a family Bible and that Gram did have her own favorite desk. Mom called my great uncle, who had the desk and the family Bible. He reluctantly looked in it and found the prayer that my grandmother had described.

The experience of losing a child and seeing my deceased grandmother taught me to know and trust my own knowing. I had awakened my gifts when I almost drowned as a two-year-old, and now, as a young mother who had lost a child, I could no longer deny the truth that I was psychic and meant to be on earth to be of service to others. Today, I have a practice that I call Metaphysical Mothering; I give Reiki soul attunements and help people clarify their karmic situations in order to heal past wounds and develop to their fullest potential.

~ *Rhobbin Alexis*

Not Perfect

A chink in the armor
A tender 'Achilles Heel'
A mortal vulnerability
In our suits of polished steel

Yes, we all have our failings
There's a runt in every litter
Who's oft the most cherished
Life's a brew of sweet and bitter

But the trick, I guess, is seeing
What's inside the chain mail
For by looking deep into the Truth
We find success each time we fail

And though the rain makes the stream
That to the mighty river runs
In turn the river meets the sea
And the water is just one

The One behind the whole of Life
IT is the source of All
And it is into ITS gentle arms
We tumble when we fall

~ *Janine Gwendoline Smith*

The Stonecutter's Message

I sat at my desk, discouraged that my work wasn't as busy as I'd hoped. A brand new doctor, I was working hard to build my practice, so the lull was disappointing. However, when I walked out of my office to take a break, I ran smack into one of my patients as she ran out the door, saying, "I'm sorry—I've waited thirty minutes and can't wait any longer. I'll call you."

Shocked, I went up to the front desk and found out that our receptionist had somehow failed to tell me that I had patients waiting. The only two I had scheduled that morning had left because they couldn't wait! I worked in a large chiropractic office at the time, and being the new doctor in the clinic, I was lowest on the totem pole.

Feeling downtrodden, frustrated, angry and confused, I thought, "Jeez! Like it's not hard enough to build a practice without having a flaky receptionist!" I felt that all my efforts to build my business were fruitless. I even considered going home for the day to have a good cry! Immersed in self pity, I glanced up at a motivational calendar on my desk and read the following:

> *When nothing seems to help,*
> *I go and watch the stonecutter,*
> *hammering away at his rock*
> *perhaps a hundred times without*
> *as much as a crack showing in it.*

Yet at the hundred and first blow,
it splits in two, and I know that it
was not that blow that did it,
but all that had gone before.[1]

I read it again—and then again. I got it! Wow! As I arose from my desk with a renewed sense of purpose, the phone started ringing, and I went forth to have a happy and productive day!

Since then, twenty years have passed, and I've had many opportunities to embrace the stonecutter's message over the years. He reminds me that life is a process—all that I do today plants seeds for tomorrow's fruit. As I water those seeds with a mixture of hope and love, life becomes juicy and ripe with purpose, creativity, and joy.

~ *Sheryl Valentine*

Whistling Mozart

*Your vision will become clear only when you look
into your heart. Who looks outside, dreams.
Who looks inside, awakens.*
— Carl Jung

Mike spit a wad of chewing tobacco into the paper-recycling bin before answering my question. "You want it today? Well, it ain't gonna happen, sweetheart."

I was expecting a surly response. That's exactly what I got.

As the vice president of a commercial printing company, one of my many tasks was to set up and maintain the work flow. The staff was always responsive to the daily assignments I posted, with the exception of the men in the pressroom. They were endlessly resistant and combative.

Forget the fact that they participated in Civil War re-enactments, hunted deer for sport, spoke primarily in 'four-letter' words, and chewed tobacco—activities that were not exactly a part of my lifestyle. Nevertheless, I'd always prided myself on being able to find some sort of common ground with all people. The men of the press-room should have been no exception. Granted, I was a woman in a man's world. But hadn't we gotten past that yet—after all, this was the 21st century, wasn't it?

On days when I felt strong and committed, I managed to crawl through the pressroom briar patch with minimal damage to my psyche. Other days, when I was worn down for one reason or another, their abusiveness was particularly stinging.

I tried every management technique ever spelled out on the printed page. Neither reward nor punishment had any effect. They were impervious to goal setting, pleading, and cajoling. Whatever I tried, the pressroom clique continued to do their jobs on their own terms, terms that were non-responsive to customer demands and that siphoned off company profits.

After work on one particularly wintry evening, I rode home with my husband in relative silence. Short of firing them all—an act that would hurt in the short term—I honestly, truly, didn't know how to bring the situation around for the good of the whole.

I bypassed supper that night and crawled into bed with a bowl of popcorn. Almost immediately, I fell into a deep sleep. It wasn't long before I found myself in a lucid dream. I was back in the pressroom.

At first, everything appeared as it did during the normal workday. All the presses were running, each with its own sound, its own recognizable rhythm. A fan set high in the wall struggled to remove the familiar smells of inks and solvents. As always, the air was white with offset powder and cigarette smoke.

When a 300 PSI air compressor suddenly roared to life, I was startled in my dream body. Regaining my composure, I squinted my eyes and slowly turned a 360-degree circle as I looked for my nemeses. Silently, I dared the pressmen to show themselves.

They began to appear, one by one, from behind a half-a-block-long press. The breath was sucked from me as I beheld the beauty of each and every one of them. They were in their Soul bodies, their true essence, the reality behind the mask of the physical form we each occupy. They were like brilliant stars of white light.

Was that love I felt? From me? From them?

I awoke the next morning and quickly cleaned up the remnants of the toppled popcorn bowl. With the dream fresh in my mind, I went about my morning rituals with images of these sparkling Souls flooding my inner screen.

That day in the pressroom was a new day. The men responded to my usual queries with a series of *No problem, I'll get right on It,* and *Sure, we can make that happen.*

What had changed? The pressmen? No, it was my attitude that was different, my perception of who and what they were.

People reflect back at us what we hold them to be. Without realizing it, I had been holding them in a mold. When I'd been shown that they weren't what I had perceived them to be—a bunch of hard-as-nails, uncooperative, redneck press jockeys—life changed for all of us. Oh sure, they still had the personalities they manifested, but they were also, like all of us, far more than that—they were Souls. Life in the pressroom was not always perfect after *the dream,* but it had changed considerably because *I* saw with new eyes.

Months later, I arrived at work early one morning to find Bud, once the surliest of the lot, whistling Mozart as he went about his press maintenance routine. *Oh, Brother! Mozart, of all things! What a contradiction!* With a self-reprimand, I quickly shut down that thought stream as the Bud of my dream flashed through my consciousness. He had been the brightest of the bright stars. Bud waved a *Good Morning* as I moved through the pressroom. I waved in return. Happily, I went about my work, a whistled rendition of Mozart sweetly echoing in my head.

~ *Jo Leonard*

The Unfolding of a Secret World

We need to be willing to let our intuition guide us, and then be willing to follow that guidance directly and fearlessly.
— Shakti Gawain

I was in communication with spirit teachers from a very early age. When you are young, it is considered cute to have "imaginary friends," but as a teen it can prove uncomfortable for all concerned. This was definitely the case for my mother and me. My mother told me constantly not to tell anyone what I saw and heard from my spirit friends. However, she loved to have me pull the dark energy away from her head so that her migraine headaches would go away. While her advice to keep quiet was probably good from a practical point of view, the implication in my mind was that if word got out, I would be a terrible blight to the family. Probably no one would come to our grocery store. The extended family wouldn't speak to us. And worst of all, we might get kicked out of the church.

This fear around the damage my secret life could impart became so strong that I shared no inner thoughts or feelings, and certainly none of the information I was given from the "other side." People just assumed I was very shy. While I didn't share, I did observe. I observed how the energy around people changed when they lied. I could tell by looking at their energy field when they were going to get sick. I sensed when individuals were genuine with me and when they were not. All this was recorded in my secret memory box.

I observed patterns that people acted out as well as their energy resonance. It was very confusing to me why certain people acted the way they did, and why they spent so much time judging others' behavior. I just couldn't understand why it wasn't clear to everyone what was real and what was fake. I somehow knew that I could perceive what most people couldn't. Yet some patterns were so obviously a misfit with the truth that I was left baffled by the lack of awareness that seemed rampant.

In the little town where I grew up, the Baptist Church was the only respectable church to attend. The others were all looked down on. This was especially true for the Assembly of God Church because their members spoke in tongues. Even though I was a member of the Baptist Church, I loved to sneak into the revival services of the Assembly of God to listen to words that were totally strange to my ears but made perfect sense to me—they rang of truth! Those people were proclaimed unreal, and yet I saw very little light around the individuals proclaiming against the revivalists. In fact, in all my years in the Baptist Church, there was only one minister whose aura got brighter when he preached, but no one seemed to notice but me.

And only three people in the little town where I grew up ever had a big light emanating from them. This was very disappointing to me. I wanted to fan the little light within everyone and make it big, but at that point I didn't know how. So I just continued to listen to my spirit teachers and observe. In fact, if it had not been for them I would have probably given up on life, but instead I made my life a study and my heart a refuge.

I had two spirit entities who taught me, and one who held me in love. The one who taught me what to do with the energies I saw came to me as a very large American Indian. There was also a teacher that came to me in the form of a Hawk. He would sit on my shoulder and teach me beautiful truths. The spirit being who held me in love never spoke a word. She was so ephemeral that often I could only feel her and not see her.

There were also people in human bodies that I learned from. I remember well one elderly lady in human form who touched my heart like no one else. She was very poor, talked with a lisp, and seemingly had no friends. Those three things would normally appear to be points against her, but she never considered them so. She was totally filled with love. She shared generously from her little bit of physical belongings and money. She had great appreciation and gratitude for exchanges of what I called "realness." And probably the most amazing thing was that she never, ever complained. I pondered often what made her different from the rest. It wasn't until I graduated from the level of observer to the level of heart resonator that I understood what made the difference.

I also had no idea at the time how all the questions that were forming as I observed what was happening around me would later become a powerful force for action. While these questions were being formed within my psyche, so were some unhealthy, separating patterns of relating that would also have to be addressed later. While it was good that I was developing a watcher self that served me internally as well as externally, it was not good that I was keeping my internal self so isolated from others. Oh, I had "friends," and I dated, but I never, ever shared my internal self. It wasn't until later in life that I found a place to share myself when I began working with my students and other healers who went about the business of bringing spiritual light to this planet.

When I attended college, I took along my observer self as well as my patterns of isolation. I ate with people and talked with classmates, but my spirit life I kept secreted away deep within me. I never questioned its reality, but it did make me feel as if I was very weird. Of course, fear that I would be found out was still hanging around. No longer did I fear for my family. Now it was about what would happen to me. I was certain I would be ridiculed and maybe even kicked out of college. So I worked hard and kept quiet!

Marriage came and went without the poor man ever having a clue whom he had married. However, the two children that came out of that marriage had psychic gifts just like mine. Since I saw their psychic abilities as wonderful parts of who they were, I was able to start healing the feelings of weirdness that I had carried with me most of my life. Thus when my spirit teachers came to me and told me it was time to do what they had been preparing me for, I was only 80% resistant rather than 100%. The thought of sharing my inner world with complete strangers was terrifying. I valiantly tried to shut my psychic eyes and ears to my spirit teachers, but I had given them too much space within me to close all the doors. Finally, from a place of exhaustion, I surrendered to the wisdom, power, love, and support they were offering to me if I would just become their channel.

People started coming to me from everywhere. Many just wanted questions answered or problems solved, but there were a good number that were willing to let me fan the light within them to a brighter hue and a bigger size. Making lights brighter and bigger was what I had always wanted to do. It was very exciting! However, I didn't know how to turn away the ones who just wanted quick fixes. So after several years of working with people with whom I could have no resonance and no return, I ended up drained and unable to enjoy life.

In July of 1990, I created a car accident that put me out of work for six months, but pulled me through my dilemma. Six months was the exact amount of time I needed to re-evaluate what I was doing and why I was doing it. I returned to my practice determined to work only with people who were willing to become students of their inner worlds and who had a deep desire to grow their light.

This began a whole new phase. I started teaching classes in addition to my psychic energy work. With tools now available for reaching inward in order to make outward changes, my students began taking giant steps forward. I now had to provide only support. I no longer had to carry them. That change, as well as choosing to work only with people who wanted their light to grow, allowed my physical and emotional vitality to come back quickly.

The years since the accident have been amazing and thrilling. Many of the questions formulated in that young girl's mind have been answered, but still a few are left hovering. I guess the biggest unanswered question is about the choices people make to live in darkness. For example, why do people choose to copy the thoughts, lifestyle, and even the feeling patterns that have been handed down through their family for generations, which leave no room for their real expression? Is continuity that important to people? I see non-fitting patterns equaling only empty, dark spaces. I may never have an answer to that kind of choice, but I am delighted to interact with more and more people who are choosing to expand their light.

My secret world is no longer a secret. I am sharing it through writing, teaching, lecturing, radio and television interviews, working with other healers, and one-on-one psychic energy sessions. I have helped hundreds of students both to discover their secret inner worlds and to share them. It feels freeing and uplifting to be able to openly express all that has been given to me.

~ *Jackie Wood*

Prayer of Commitment

To you, Lord, I give my dreams,
I give you all that I am.
Every part of me is yours,
my life is in your hands.

Lord, I give you everything
that first you gave to me,
my gifts, my talents, good and bad,
the best and worst of me.

You are the Potter,
I am the clay.
Mold me. Make me yours
in every way.

Change me, change my heart.
Transform me, Lord I pray.
For now and through Eternity.
My life I give today.

~ *Nell M. Berry*

Spiritual Designs

Never so act, in any manner, in any inclination, that there
may ever be an experience of regret within the self.
Let the moves and the discourteousness, the unkindness,
all come from the other. Better to be abased ...
and have the peace within! ... act ever in the way ye would
like to be acted toward. No matter what others say or even
do, do as ye would be done by; and then the peace
that has been promised is indeed thine own.
— Edgar Cayce

It was spring 2005 when I met with some colleagues over a business dinner. In my job as president of a fashion design company, I had worked with these individuals over the years in various transactions. We talked a lot about the fashion business and at one point they asked me, "What gives you so much inspiration in life? You always appear so happy and full of energy. You inspire us, and we look forward to getting together with you."

I thought for a second and said, "I get my inspiration simply from giving of myself to others."

They were silent for a moment and then someone said, "You come across to us as a person whose life is so easy. You are very strong. We see you getting all the best things in life like a husband who brings home a lot of money, a great job, and a big house. It seems as though you never have to suffer, that you don't have any idea of the suffering and struggle in life. Tell us more."

I kept silent, for it was somewhat funny. I didn't want to spoil the illusion. What they saw on the outside was like a duck on the water: calm on top, but paddling like mad underneath. My days were a constant struggle, a balancing act between many crises in my work, home, and family. There were some serious health issues to deal with as well. But each day I put on my uniform of clothes and make-up and went out into the world, trying to make it a better place for all.

And in spite of all the difficulties and stresses in my life, there were even more blessings than the ones my colleagues had described. These blessings came from the protection of Spirit helping me with the challenges that had come my way.

For example, a couple of major accounts had been with my company for over ten years, but lately the pressure from outside competition had made holding onto these accounts a challenge. So much so, the survival of my company was threatened.

To make matters worse, one of these companies had had a big management shake-up. Most of the senior vice presidents and managers, including buyers that had previously worked with me, had been fired, and new people had been assigned their positions. Where once I'd had comfortable, warm relationships, I was back to having to prove myself and my company all over again.

That spring, I was called in for a big presentation of my latest product line. The new managers wanted me to convince them of the reasons that they should stay with my company. They let me know they had the same sources as I had and therefore didn't need a middleman.

The first couple of hours went well. Their VP of Designs absolutely loved what I presented for the 2006 season. But when the new vice president arrived later, things turned sour. A hard core company person, she was determined to show her boss she was in control.

Everything I tried to show her met with pessimism. In fact, she told me right there in front of her entire staff that I really wasn't needed. Devastated, I envisioned millions of dollars going out the door. I knew there was a real possibility that without their business, we would not be able to sustain ours.

I stood there thinking really fast. If I confronted her, she would use it against me and surely kill the business. For some reason she was on a real power trip. It seemed something about me was provoking her. So I took a deep breath and waited for a signal from my inner guide. Inwardly I asked, 'What should I do?' There I stood, in the conference room full of clients, inwardly singing the HU, an ancient name for God. HU is a prayer that opens the heart and allows one to hear the voice of God. It seemed like minutes, but it took only a few seconds.

Suddenly, a warm feeling of love entered my heart, and I felt very calm. A feeling of absolute surrender came over me. I turned to my colleagues and asked them to take all the presentation boards down, pack up our designs, and prepare to leave. At that point, my heart was truly filled with love. I looked into the vice president's eyes and saw a deep unhappiness in her. I looked at her non-judgmentally and saw that she didn't love herself. I noticed she was having difficulty keeping eye contact with me. She couldn't bear the love that was flowing through me. This truth was very clear to me, and therefore I could not get angry or fire back at her. Instead I simply said, "I think I've done all I can in here. It's time for me to wrap it up. I wish you all the best in making the right choices and selections for your 2006 season and hope you enjoy great benefits from it."

Silence followed. You could cut the air with a knife.

I saw her struggling for a moment and then she said, "I think we should look at a couple of pieces and maybe consider them."

"No problem," I said, "Please do." The managers began pulling out one collection after another, and before long they expressed a genuine interest in half my entire line. It felt like I'd just woken up from a bad dream. Suddenly, from all that animosity and rejection I had moved to not only acceptance, but even some respect? Now that's what I call Spirit in action.

The love that poured out of me for the vice president had reshaped the entire meeting. The company did indeed order, and since that time our relationship has healed and deepened.

No matter what difficulties we face, when we remember to put Spirit first in our lives, it can create miracles where before there were none.

~ *Teresa Miller*

Is It True, Necessary, and Kind?

As supervising hostess of the Churchill Valley Country Club, my job was to keep things running smoothly. I was in charge of overseeing the wait staff for five separate dining rooms, as well as keeping an eye on the salad department and the chefs in the kitchen.

One particular waitress and chef could not get along. For the sake of their privacy I will call the waitress Rita and the chef Roy. The executive chef scheduled the cooks, and I scheduled the wait staff, so it was impossible to avoid encounters between Rita and Roy, as I had no authority over the cooks.

The least little thing would set them off, so the shouting matches were frequent. Asking them to tone it down, warning them that their jobs were at stake, and hoping for the best just wasn't enough. Something had to be done, but what?

I knew I had to take steps to clear up this constant confrontation and bickering. Because I often use dreams to solve life's problems, I knew I should "sleep on it." That night, as I prepared for bed, I did a technique where I visualized sitting at a round blue table with my inner guide, and I explained to him the entire situation.

Both Rita and Roy excelled in their jobs, I said, and I wouldn't want to lose them. I asked for instructions on how to help them see the error of their ways without my interfering with their right to make choices. Then I asked for a dream of guidance that would help alleviate the situation at work by saying, "I invite you to help me, help them in accordance with thy will and not mine."

That night I had a lucid dream. The setting was the boardroom of the country club where Rita, Roy, and I were seated at a round table with a white tablecloth. I was in the middle, Rita to my far left, and Roy to the side on my right. They made sure there was a lot of distance between us.

Then I said, "There is a technique I want to try called, "*Is it true, necessary and kind?*" I don't remember what was said during the dream, but it ended with us sitting together on the same side of the table and laughing together.

The next morning I set the stage to play out the dream with Rita and Roy. After lunch, there are several hours during which the wait staff and chefs prepare for the dinner guests. During this slow period I approached Rita and Roy separately and asked them to attend a private meeting where we could come to some sort of solution for this situation and bring harmony. They both scoffed at the suggestion, but agreed to join me in the boardroom for a meeting that I hoped would end as happily as my dream had.

I went into the boardroom alone before the scheduled time of the meeting. The table was round and was covered with a white cloth, just like the dream. I silently sang HU. HU is a sacred name for God that I use not to change things, but to raise my state of consciousness to be in alignment with Divine Spirit.

Roy and Rita came in separately. The seating arrangements were exactly the same as in the dream. Rita was in the middle of the table to my left, and Roy was in the middle of the table to my right. I was experiencing deja vu. I knew at that instant whatever happened would be in the best interests of all of us. I felt relaxed, confident, and loved.

Looking at them, I said firmly but gently, "Rita, in the next five minutes I want you to tell Roy what it is about him that upsets you so much. And Roy, please refrain from saying anything until Rita is finished."

For the next few minutes they poured out their anger and resentment for each other. Some of the language used was so foul it polluted the air. I could actually feel the discordant vibrations. After each had expressed their feelings, we sat quietly for a moment. "Rita, Roy," I said with as much love as I could muster up, "Is what you said about each other true?"

"Most of it," replied Rita.

"Well," Roy said, scratching his chin, "I guess I did exaggerate some things about her."

My next question was, "Was it necessary to say these things to each other?"

Roy looked not at me but directly at Rita. "You do have a way of pushing my buttons." Then he turned to me. "I guess I just say things to hurt her even if they aren't necessary."

Rita was taken aback by his honesty. "The same goes for me too."

My last question was, "Was it kind to say these things to each other?"

"What's kind got to do with it? I don't like working with Roy, so I don't want to be nice to him," answered Rita.

When I asked her why she truly didn't like him, it took her a few seconds before she answered. "He acts like he knows everything. He's arrogant!"

Roy's rebuttal was, "Oh! What about you, Miss Know-It-All?"

I smiled. "You know, you both are so much alike. You are like siblings trying to outdo each other for the favor of whomever it is you are trying to please."

The word sibling was said without thinking. I knew at that moment the past life they had shared together was as brother and sister.

"Just who is it you are trying to impress?" I asked them. They didn't have an answer. I gave them a moment to think about one last thing they wanted to air out before the meeting ended. Neither had anything to say.

I requested that they shake hands and in the future agree to disagree more agreeably. I thanked them for their candor, and they thanked me for the opportunity to get so many things off their chests about each other.

In spite of our meeting, Rita and Roy were back at it the very next day, but a subtle change had occurred. They weren't quite as loud, and the words were not as harsh. At least that was a step in the right direction.

Gradually their behavior took a turn for the better. One day when I went into the kitchen to check on an order, I overheard Roy say, not with the usual loud voice, but with an assertive tone, "Rita, stop pushing my buttons."

"Hey, I like pushing your buttons, don't you know that by now?" she asked. Then she added, "It's about time you got new buttons. Just once I'd like to suggest something about your cooking that you would agree on."

"Hey, if you can do better, get behind this counter and let me see what you can do under the pressure of ten waitresses complaining about one thing or another."

I didn't detect anger, just annoyance about the situation.

"I would, except I don't want to wear them stupid checkered pants," she responded, laughing at the black and white checked pants all the chefs wore with white jackets and white hats.

He looked up from the plate he was preparing, "You think I look bad. Take a look in the mirror! You look like a penguin." The waitresses wore black jumpers with white shirts. As they looked at each other, a strange sound started to emerge. Laughter! They both were laughing. I began laughing too.

The dream I had about the meeting with them came to mind. I remembered that in the dream we were sitting together laughing. Now here we all were, standing together laughing.

And that was not the only incredible change I was to witness.

The first time I heard Rita pay a compliment to Roy's cooking I was flabbergasted, to say the least. The clincher for me was when Roy asked Rita to taste test a new recipe he was planning to put on the menu. These two former opponents were becoming allies at work.

When Roy left to open his own restaurant, he even asked Rita to come and work for him. He had come to the realization that Rita was a great waitress. Rita declined with a thank you, and she is still working at the Country Club to this day. As for me, I am retired from the restaurant business now, but I am still learning to give and receive love as Soul, a divine spark of God.

~ *Betty Jane Rapin*

Flying to Heaven

Service is the rent we pay for being.
It is the very purpose of life,
and not something you do in your spare time.
— Marian Wright Edelman

I had a recurring dream for many years. *It is World War ll. I am married to a fighter pilot, a man whom I loved very deeply. He was shot down over enemy territory in Europe. As years passed, I would often hear his voice whispering in the background: "Tell them it's O.K. And I will always love you. Love overcame the fear."*

For some reason, this dream gave me tremendous reassurance that I was following my life's calling, aligning my work values with my spiritual values. I had never had any ambition to be a flight attendant. I stumbled upon this "dream career" quite by chance. But then again, I am always reminded that destiny does not need a reason.

I had burned out as a massage therapist. Flying was to be a temporary respite, but it kept calling me back. What was it about leaving terra firma, rising above the clouds, and almost touching heaven that made my heart sing? What was so familiar about all this?

In quiet contemplation one day, I realized that I had made a commitment to serve this lifetime humbly and in whatever fashion it might be. Among my many responsibilities as a flight attendant is the traveling public's safety and well-being. Post 9/11, I have noticed an increased level of stress and apprehension on the part of some travelers: white knuckles gripping the armrest, sometimes profuse sweating, and other symptoms of fear of flying.

Perhaps because of my past experience in the healing profession, I seem to have a knack for calming and reassuring these frightened souls. Although I speak with them very calmly as if to distract them, I am also having an inner conversation with them on another level. I am reminding them: I made a commitment to accompany you; I will not abandon you; I will travel with you to your destination; You will not be alone; You will be safe; and I will take care of you, I promise. By the end of the flight, they may still dislike flying, but they will have overcome a certain degree of fear and have gained some self-confidence.

For eighteen years the sky has been my home.

I often tell myself that to serve another human being is, in essence, to serve God. My journey home has taken many twists, turns and detours. But as long as I remember to honor my commitment to you, my fellow travelers, I will always be happy in knowing that my career is also in service to God.

~ *Sylvia Jong*

5

The Courage to Believe

Will today be the day you decide once and for all to make your life consistent with the quality of your spirit? Then start by proclaiming, "This is what I am. This is what my life is about. And this is what I'm going to do. Nothing will stop me from achieving my destiny. I will not be denied!"

— *Awaken the Giant Within*
by Anthony Robbins

A Dream of Destiny

Trust the dreams, for in them is hidden the gate to eternity.
— Kahlil Gibran

I was on the phone with a close friend that afternoon sharing insights and ideas about life and our spiritual viewpoint. At one point in the conversation my friend asked me to hold on, saying, "I want to read you something important." I listened with great interest to a short paragraph about a spiritual principle of particular significance to me. After she finished, I said, "Wow, that was amazing. Who wrote that?"

"You did," she answered.

It was my custom to scribble ideas and thoughts as they came to me. For a short time I had stayed with my friend and must have left the pages somewhere, not thinking they were of any importance. But this hadn't been the first time a wake-up call had come to say, writing is your destiny.

In the year 1990, I awakened from a dream that was to be pivotal and painful. A circle of geese was spinning at a supersonic rate of speed. My spiritual guide came and took one goose from the circle and pulled a feather from its throat.

The following morning, I awoke with a phantom pain around my throat. It felt like a band or strap was fastened around my throat, and it was quite uncomfortable. After the dream, my life changed dramatically. I lost touch with my intuition. It was as if my own inner voice was walled away from me. I lost the ability to read for pleasure or even for comfort. It was as if the words scrambled on the page. And a great depression came over me.

I began looking for answers to the dream's meaning and purpose in my life, but for almost two years nothing came. Then one night I dreamt I was in a Chinese herb store. I walked up to the counter and asked a woman there, "What's wrong with me?"

"You have an Eastern Parasite," she said.

The next morning, even more confused and with still another dream to unravel, I felt some relief that at least I had a piece of the puzzle.

During that time, I had a dream with Oprah Winfrey, in which she handed me a snake. She had begun to appear randomly, in each dream advising me on how I was doing in my training. She had clearly taken me on as a student. But of what I wasn't certain.

Then in 1993, I organized an event for a group of approximately 200 called The Sacred Hand of God. We had invited a guest speaker, a writer and gifted spiritual teacher. That evening, during dinner, as I sat with a group of the seminar attendees, a great nausea overtook me. I tried to gain composure, but a feeling of hysteria caused me to call out to the group and ask if we could leave the restaurant. Fortunately, we were at the end of our meal and were able to pay the check and leave quite quickly. As we left the restaurant, someone from our group suggested we go across the street for a coffee. I followed along passively because one of the group had the keys to the car which would bring us back to the seminar some distance away.

I sat on a bench, the nausea spiking to a level where I felt it would overcome me. I counseled myself to stay calm, relax, let go … Finally, the band of nausea across my stomach released as if I were giving birth. Then in the next moment, a great realization came over me. The meaning of the dream of the circle of geese was revealed to me. At the same time I remembered too, that that evening I was to tell a story on a panel I myself had organized, and which I had forgotten about during the hectic schedule of that day. I knew I was to talk about the dream and its meaning.

It was revealed that the feather in the goose's throat was a quill, a tool for writing … I knew that I had come to this life to write, and that this was what I had spent all of my life moving toward. This had shown up as a passion for reading and writing as early as five years old. That evening I told the story. I'm sure that most in attendance had no idea of the magnitude of how this dream had altered my life.

But in spite of the revelation that evening, I still felt far from healed. The dreams with Oprah continued. She came to advise me on how I was moving forward in my life. It was as if I were in training to be like her, or to achieve a potential that had been agreed to before this life. She seemed to represent my highest ideal.

Sometimes she would chastise me for how I had handled some aspect of my life. If I tried to take on too much, a dream would show me being the producer of her show as well as the lighting person, literally trying to do the whole show myself. A life lesson to delegate was obvious.

Then in 1994, I was out of a job. I had been working as a publicist on a short-term assignment, and now I found myself out of work shortly before Christmas. With few options in sight, I sat down to visualize the life of my dreams. In my imagination I guided an inner paintbrush and began painting the life I'd envisioned. I painted the bluest skies and the most beautiful path through a breathtaking landscape. I breathed life into it through every cell in my being, and then I let it go.

The next day, I met with a friend. She asked me what I was doing for living, and I told her of my publicity work. She asked me what a publicist does, and I told her: we help others to publicize their books or products in the media. She asked, "Do you think you could help me solicit stories for a book I'm compiling?" And I said, "Why not?"

Very soon after I found myself working full time collecting stories for two of the *Chicken Soup for the Soul* books. My short publicity campaign had been so successful that my friend had hired me, first on a part-time basis, then on a full-time basis. After a year we had developed the manuscript for our first book. It was to contain 110 stories, each graded by readers from 1-10: 10 being, "I love the story. It made me cry. It's the best story I've ever read and gave me goose bumps, tears." Ratings of 1-7 would never get into the book. Just not good enough.

We handed in the manuscript but discovered we were short 20 stories of a 10 grade. My associate said, "Take off your publicist hat. You're a writer now. Go out and get us stories!" The next day I was in a local bookstore searching for ideas when I found a book called *Living with the End in Mind* by Erin and Doug Kramp. The book was written by a couple who had appeared on Oprah several times in the last few years. Erin had been diagnosed with cancer, and she was building a legacy for her daughter Peyton to leave behind when she passed away. Erin and Doug had videotaped an extensive series of videos with lessons about growing up, from "How to put on make-up" and "How to cook spaghetti," to "What to do when you meet your first boyfriend." As well, Erin wrote a letter for every year up to Peyton's 16th birthday, with a charm in each so that by the time she was 16 the bracelet would be complete.

I had watched this story unfolding on TV and decided to contact the couple to ask them to write a piece for *Chicken Soup for the Parent's Soul*, one of the books we were compiling. Almost immediately, I was on the phone with Doug Kramp, interviewing him about the story. Two hours later, I hung up the phone and sobbed uncontrollably for ten minutes. The story was so powerful and life altering, I couldn't get control of myself.

Doug told me how at one point two years after she was diag-nosed, Erin was so ill from an infection that the doctor told him she might die very soon. While her body fought for life, her spirit was in another place, and she began a spiritual journey. During her experience, Erin later told Doug that she came in contact with a white light and was told her real purpose in life. She became aware that her life's simple purpose was just to let God's love flow through her.

When she did recover, she knew that she had to quit her job and dedicate all her spare time to her daughter and most importantly, to being a channel for love. She knew that this was all that mattered. So for the next few years, she educated Peyton about the circle of life. One afternoon, Peyton brought a cicada bug shell into the house. Erin used that as an opportunity to explain the separation of spirit and body. She showed her how the shell was empty, and the body that had been there had just left the shell behind. She explained that when we die, only the shell of our bodies is left. Our spirit leaves and travels to its true home in heaven. Erin told Peyton how her great-grand-mother was there and her great-great grandmother, as well as all the relatives who had died previously. "And one day, Peyton, I too will leave this body and go to heaven," Erin explained. "Peyton, you'll be a part of the circle of life as well," and Peyton understood.

One evening in early October, four years after the original diagnosis, Erin started declining. A hospital bed was brought into Doug and Erin's home and put next to a big picture window on the main floor. Doug was with Erin, holding her hand, when she saw the white light again. They realized that Erin's time was short and that they would have to talk to Peyton soon.

On October 30, Erin woke from a nap with a brightness and clarity she hadn't had for some time. Doug went to get Peyton from her room upstairs so that she could say goodbye to her mother. Before he went, he jotted down some words on a piece of paper to recall the lessons they had painstakingly taught Peyton. Words like, cicada shell, the circle of life, and angel, all to help him with what he knew he had to say. Pushing open Peyton's door, he told her they needed to go see Mom. Once they entered the den, Peyton jumped up on the bed to snuggle with Erin. The two were smiling and cuddling though Erin wasn't strong enough to do a lot of talking.

Then Doug told Peyton, "Mom's getting ready to go to heaven. It's her time very soon." Peyton cried and Erin cried, but you could see that Peyton understood. That fact was so important to Doug and Erin.

Erin passed away Halloween morning at 4:00 a.m. The next morning Doug woke up to a voice that said, "God's love, God's love, God's love!" and he felt a great force of light and love flowing into him so strongly he could hardly stand it. Then the next moment it stopped, and Doug felt Erin come up behind him and put her arms around him as another surge of love came through and then subsided.

The very first night after Erin died, Peyton was praying and said, "Mom, I know you're up in heaven and you're having a great time. We thank you for Halloween because it's going to be a double holiday from now on. It's going to be a day when we always get candy, and it's a day that we'll get to celebrate you getting to heaven."

One day when Doug was missing Erin, he said to Peyton, "You know what, Peyton, I really missed Mom today."

Peyton looked at him and said, "Why, Dad? She's been with us all day long."

I submitted the story after transcribing the interview. After some editing it became our lead story from then on. We soon had a full manuscript, and *Chicken Soup for the Parent's Soul* went on to become a best seller.

That same night after interviewing Doug, I had my final dream with Oprah. She pulled up in a white limousine and stepped out wearing a beautiful suit. Then she turned to me and said, "You can have your suit back now!"

When I awoke, I knew I had finally met the agreement I'd made before I came to this life. I'd done what Oprah had been calling me to do from the first dream when she handed me the snake. I later discovered that in American Indian medicine the snake is a symbol for true wealth and transformation.

It's some years later, and I'm on my fourth book. I've taken up the challenge and stepped fully into my life mission. I've learned a lot more about animal medicine and how images and dreams of animals, insects, and birds can be powerful omens of our life path. Long after the realization of my goose dream, another vital piece came to me through a friend who had read my first book, *Dream Yourself Awake,* where I talked at length about that dream. The piece she sent was this:

The appearance of Goose means two things most commonly; I need to pay more attention to myths and stories as they begin to appear in my life, and something needs changing—a new possibility is beginning to open up in my life and a whole new "map" is needed to navigate it. I need to prepare to embark on a new "quest." The Universe is always speaking to us through an infinite variety of sources. Stories and myths, signs and omens, intuition, something someone says on the bus as we are heading into work, the program that comes on the television which is exactly what you needed to see at the moment you turned it on.

Each dream we have is embedded with many levels of truth and wisdom. A dream can unfold over time to reveal its layers and deeper meanings. I learned that Goose medicine people are the storytellers of our time. They are here to gather stories that tell of our purpose here on this planet. All those years ago my goose dream had shown me my life mission. And the snake dream held the other piece of the puzzle. Oh yes, the eastern parasite story is in my first book, *Dream Yourself Awake.* If you'd like to know the ending, please read it ...

The answers to why you're here are in your dreams. I now live my mission fully, and you can too!

~ *Darlene Montgomery*

The Power of Gratitude

I work at my husband's medical clinic and have the incredible privilege of seeing his patients begin the healing process right in front of my eyes. My husband is a medical doctor who practices holistic medicine, advising his patients in the use of proper nutrition and supplements, and healthy lifestyle changes. He treats not just the physical body, but all aspects of a person. Illness can result from emotional, mental, or even spiritual distress.

After my husband analyzes a patient's history, rechecks the results of the physical exam, and checks the results of any tests that were performed, he writes up a program for healing. My job is to explain his instructions and try to make them as easy to follow as I can. Initially, patients can be very anxious, frightened, and overwhelmed. A very important part of this treatment is to reduce stress as much as possible.

Joe, a Vietnam veteran, had been told by his oncologist that his cancer was terminal, and he should go home and get his affairs in order. This is his story.

After explaining his nutritional program, I started to give him self-healing exercises. The first one was gratitude.

"Upon awakening," I told him, "before you open your eyes in the morning, begin to give thanks, individually, for each thing that you are grateful for in your life. This moves your attention away from what you do not want in your life and places it on what you do want. This also takes energy away from what is unwanted and places it on what is wanted. People have a tendency to dwell on the negative instead of the positive."

Joe told me emphatically, "I ain't grateful for nothing!"

I asked, "Can you see me?"

"Yes," he answered.

I asked, "Can you hear me?"

Again his response was, "Yes."

"Do you now understand how to do 'The Gratitude Exercise'?" I looked at him intently. He nodded his head, a thoughtful expression on his face. I introduced the next exercise.

"Always live in the moment. The past is gone. You may have made some terrible mistakes, but you learned from them. The future is unknown; you don't want to live there, either. You want to live in the moment."

Joe began to weep. I knew then that his healing was beginning.

I reached the last exercise. "When you brush your teeth each morning and evening, look in the mirror, look in your eyes, and say, 'I love me and I forgive me.'"

Joe stared at me and said, "I hate myself, and I can't forgive myself. I could never do what you're asking me to do."

Softly, I asked him, "Is it possible that this is the reason why you are sick? Maybe you just don't love yourself enough to take care of yourself."

With tears rolling down his cheeks, he nodded.

When Joe returned six weeks later for his follow-up visit, he stopped by my office. "I'm able to love myself and forgive myself," he told me. "I have a lot to be grateful for, and I'm living in the present every day." He looked very healthy and relaxed, and his smile was beautiful.

I knew then that he would be well. And he is.

~ *Jackie Mantell*

Jana—The Beauty of Survival

Man often becomes what he believes himself to be.
If I keep on saying to myself that I cannot do a certain
thing, it is possible that I may end by really becoming
incapable of doing it. On the contrary, if I shall have
the belief that I can do it, I shall surely acquire the
capacity to do it, even if I may not have it
at the beginning.
— Mahatma Gandhi

Tears rolled down her cheeks as she glanced back at her home. Somehow she knew this was the end and that she would not return. As she crept through the darkness towards the river, whispers echoed in the distance. Straining to see who was boarding the boat, she witnessed teenage girls with bandages wrapped around the stumps that were once their legs. Jana was barefoot, but at least she had feet. "Why do we have war?" she asked no one in particular. Grabbing the plastic bag that contained all the personal belongings she could take with her, she escaped Yugoslavia.

Jana Dzojic was the second child and first daughter of seven children born to a Catholic family in a Communist country. When she was very young, her father left the household to find work in Germany, returning only sporadically throughout her youth. Money was scarce because Catholics weren't given the favor of work that could buy food and clothing. Life was difficult, yet they survived. As each child graduated high school, he knew he had to leave Croatia to survive. Jana, who had been a seamstress, was recruited by the civil police, taught to shoot a gun, and shown how to survive.

As the tensions of war threatened, people disappeared, never to be seen again. Soon it was brother against brother, and blood began to color the landscape. With all her family already gone to Germany, Jana knew that if she didn't cross the Sava River that night, she might not live to see the next day.

She arrived in Germany with two skills: sewing and shooting. Although she soon fell in love with this new country, she could not find work with her refugee status. Every few weeks she had to stand in long lines that could take two days to navigate, attempting to keep her visa. Never giving up hope, she studied to be a beauty consultant. It wasn't long before she realized that making others feel beautiful on the inside and out was her calling. Her spirits soared as she offered luxurious facials, manicures, and other treatments. For awhile she was very happy.

However, no country wants refugees forever! Germany mandated that all single people were to be extradited to their homeland. The war was raging, and she would face certain death if she returned. She couldn't go back. What was she to do?

Jana had heard of a Catholic charity in Oakland, California that would purchase an airline ticket to America for refugees. She applied and was accepted with the caveat that the ticket was a loan and would be considered her first line of credit. With only the equivalent of $41 in her pocket, Jana arrived in America with no family, no contacts, and no English. In her first year she was constantly moving from place to place, attempting to find work, a room to sleep, and food to eat. Despite the desperation, Jana moved forward each day with faith, and finally she got a job paying minimum wage as a bagger for a large grocery chain. Immediately she started paying back her loan to the Catholic charity.

Saving every penny and paying her bills, she built her credit. Yet she longed to get back into the beauty business that was her heart. With a scholarship she enrolled in cosmetology school, diligently attended classes, and graduated with a big celebration. Living in small rented rooms while still working at the grocery store, she continued to take additional courses in the art of massage, facials, and other body treatments.

Within five years, Jana had achieved her dream. Not only did she speak English fluently, she had purchased a home of her own, and with the assistance of a generous landlord, she had opened an opulent and luxurious European Day Spa where clients are pampered in an elegant environment designed and crafted by her own hands. Her years of determination, suffering, and struggle had inspired her to create a retreat for others from the chaos of life.

Jana blesses America. She is overjoyed to call the United States her home. Despite the long hours and hard work, she is grateful for the opportunities that were available to her. Although she mourns the absence of her relatives, her clients and friends have become her American family. Every day she beautifies the world a bit more with her special touch, with her caring personality, and with her hopeful attitude. Every client is spoiled with the richest creams and most delicate products. She proudly serves fresh fruit, wine, tea, or other refreshments in beautiful crystal and china. European Day Spa is a place a weary soul can come to indulge the senses, relax, rejuvenate, and revive the spirit. Thank goodness Jana never gave up.

Tonight as she closes the door after a busy day, tears roll down her cheeks when she glances back at her spa. "My shop," she sighs, "my home." Somehow she knows this is just the beginning.

~ *Cynthia Brian*

From Spark to Flame

If you want your life to be more rewarding, you have to change the way you think.

— Oprah Winfrey

When my now 19-year-old daughter was in Grade 3, all of Mrs. Mathews' students were given a small pot with a bean seed to plant. Green string beans, it seems, are pretty hardy, and the perfect seed to use when promoting green thumbs in young children. That same plant was also a most unexpected source of understanding and insight for me.

Once the bean plants had sprouted and flowered, their teacher allowed the kids to carefully transfer the precious cargo from school to home. Once home, Shanna scouted around for the perfect location, finally settled on a sunny south windowsill, and then proudly declared, "Soon I can feed the whole family!"

Shanna's sisters were envious, and even our cat looked intrigued, which should have been a warning to me because when I woke up the next morning, I saw that the bean plant had been fiercely knocked off the windowsill and ripped from its pot. Its leaves were frayed and except for a limp thread of stem that still connected the roots to the flowering top, it was quite unrecognizable from the day before. The plant, it seemed, was a goner.

I dreaded what I had to tell Shanna, but as I gently began to explain that the bean plant had to be put in the compost, her reaction was not what I expected. She said, "Everything will be OK, Mom. The plant will get better."

Without wasting a second in thought, she secured the first aid kit from the bathroom, returning with gauze, a tongue depressor, bandages, and a deep belief that the pathetic-looking, near-dead bean plant would live, thrive, and even produce food!

I had mixed emotions, knowing that she was postponing the plant's inevitable trip to the compost bin, but I went along with her plan and helped her wrap bandages. Days later, to my absolute surprise, the bean plant was standing tall and looking perky. We were able to remove the bandages and discover a protruding hump in the stem where its near-fatal stem break had been. It was also amazing to see that the one and only bean had become plump, almost completely masking the claw marks that had scarred it.

I don't know why I hadn't thought the cat might go for a second round, because he surely did, and this time I was the one who ran for the first aid kit! I carefully applied a heavy blanket of everything from cotton and gauze to colored Band-aids with "Ouch" written on them. When the medic work was done, I whispered a little something to the heavens.

Just one week later we were able to take the bandages off and again we barely found evidence of an attack. There was even a new sliver of green where a second bean was forming. I was excited and amazed, while Shanna had been expecting nothing less. Back to the windowsill it went, but this time we built a fortress of heavy books to keep it safe until our day of bounty.

I set the table beautifully with all the fanfare of a Thanksgiving dinner. The beans were carefully divided by five, which awarded each person two small pieces, claw marks and all. They turned out to be the best green beans I had ever eaten!

My daughter never quite understood my exuberance over the

significance of the beans. But in my work as a youth motivator, I am brought together with kids and teens that all desperately need people to believe in them. Now, more than ever, no matter what I have been told about a child or a teen and their behavior, I see everyone, *no exceptions*, with the same eyes and heart that my daughter used on her broken, beaten-up bean plant.

I wonder if it's a coincidence that later that same week, I stumbled upon a most appropriate quote by Italian poet Dante (1265-1351): "From a little spark, may burst a mighty flame." Especially if you believe!

~ *Monique Howat*

It Started With a Dream

"Let the beauty be what we do:
There are hundreds of ways to kneel and kiss the ground."
— Rumi

Sitting in a dental chair after a lengthy session, I was surprised to hear the assistant ask me, "Are you still working?"

With my jaw still frozen, I said simply, "Yes."

She surprised me again by adding, "Do you enjoy your work?"

I immediately replied, "I love it!"

"Well," she said, "one doesn't hear that too often."

Her initial question was prompted by my age. I am 67 years of age. I have no desire to retire, but then I was a late starter. Starting a career later in life is not surprising when I reflect back on a session with a palm reader 36 years ago. As a housewife and mother, I was a co-conspirator with four friends as we gathered in a friend's home one evening to have our palms read.

I wasn't feeling so conspiratorial or cocky when I went home that evening. I was reflective and confused—the palm reader had been amazingly accurate about events in my life to that point. A prediction that I would have a fairly long period of dissatisfaction starting in my forties did not particularly bother me. With my husband, I was raising two children aged 11 and 7 years, so life seemed full. I eventually wanted a career, but that was not an immediate concern.

The palm reader experience had started as a lark, but now it triggered a serious quest. Are some events predestined? I looked anew at what I was passing along to my children. It suddenly seemed our lives were all about buying material goods. The religion of my childhood did not have answers for me, so I started searching. Four years later, I found the answers I was looking for. I was not looking for a spiritual teacher. The religion that rang truth for me, however, offered a spiritual leader—a master who taught in the inner worlds as well as on the outer. If a master came with the teachings, I decided to accept that. The turn of events in our lives soon made me grateful for the support and guidance of this gentle inner and outer master and the teachings that guided me.

As a result of an accident while playing basketball, my husband required an eye operation. Complications from that operation led to two more surgeries before he lost his sight in that eye. Then what we thought was his good eye also required an operation. Two more operations on that eye happily saved his sight. It was a traumatic few years. During this time, I returned to the workplace.

Over a span of several years, I worked as a mortgage broker, sold advertising, and sold a line of nutritional products through network marketing. I enjoyed my work but hankered for a career without knowing what that would be. A turning point came during a training session sponsored by the nutritional company. "What," we were asked, "did we most enjoy doing?" The question took me by surprise. I hadn't stepped back to think about that—ever!

An answer popped into mind quite suddenly. I loved to research and write. I had tapped into my feelings when I was immersed in searching for, reading, and digesting information; then putting findings and thoughts to paper. "This," I realized, "is what I love to do!"

My research had centered on nutrition and natural health

therapies, and my writing had been limited to letters to the editor and holiday travel reflections to share with family. Sharing information with others was an important ingredient. I had also worked as a classroom teacher before devoting my time to home and family.

Now in my forties, I wondered how I could earn a living doing what I now knew I loved to do. I wrote a weight control program, voiced it to background music, and packaged a booklet and audio-tape for direct mail marketing. I gained positive feedback from workshops based on the program, but I soon looked for other projects when it didn't sell through mail order ads.

I awoke one morning with a special memory from the dream state. I had been in a writing class with one of the spiritual masters associated with my religion. I was thrilled at his invitation to return for instruction whenever I wanted. This experience spurred me to find avenues for my desire to write. As a result, I wrote articles that were published in several magazines. Business projects gave me experience writing advertising copy and corporate letters. While I was delighted to be writing, as a freelancer I was not able to pursue my heart-interest. Natural health has become a popular subject now, but there was limited interest back then. I yearned for a career that I could feel passionate about.

Over a period of years, I applied for several positions. My resume often got me to the interview stage. At that point, I would blow it. I realized I wasn't putting my heart into the interviews because of an overwhelming feeling that the corporate world would bind me in a straightjacket. I felt frustrated, but I was also learning to trust Spirit and to listen. Through daily contemplation, my inner guidance told me I had more to learn. Then, perhaps, the right position would come my way.

With time on my hands, I wanted to volunteer my services in the community, but my self-image held me back. I felt I first needed to have meaningful work to give me necessary status on committees.

Another turning point came when I awoke from a dream with the name of a newspaper—*The Seattle Post-Intelligencer*. Since I lived in British Columbia, Canada, this was not a newspaper I normally read. I found the newspaper, however, at a specialty newsstand and set about reading it. One article grabbed my attention. It was about a health initiative that involved community volunteers. I realized I would enjoy volunteer work of this nature. Besides, encouragement from the dream state always boosts my confidence.

Within weeks, one of our local newspapers reported a call for volunteers. Our city health department was looking for residents to join a committee to spearhead a new health initiative. The provincial government was developing a system to make health care more sensitive to local needs. I applied and was accepted. I was now able to bring a voice for natural health to the table and help bring the natural health community together to conduct and publish a community-wide survey. I gained invaluable leadership skills.

Shortly after, I landed a job as public relations coordinator for the small Canadian office of a U.S. corporation. I enjoyed the work, but pervasive office politics muddied the working environment. I knew, however, I had something to learn as well as something to give, so I didn't want to leave the situation until I felt my purpose in being there had been completed. I decided to ask for a "waking dream" so I would know when to leave. A waking dream is a clue we get from life that usually comes in a form of some unusual occurrence, or symbolism in some life event.

I had been noticing that a pizza company used seven identical digits for their phone number. I decided to use numbers as the signal, but I didn't want to make it as easy as a phone number, so I set the waking dream to see six identical numbers. When I saw that sequence, it would be time to leave this job. A few months later, while working with a software program I used to compose the company newsletter, I was checking a tutorial on one aspect of the software.

I saw a row of identical numbers, but they didn't register because I was so focused on the task at hand. Before sleep that night, however, my inner voice told me I'd seen my waking dream. When I checked at work next morning, sure enough, there were six identical digits in the example I'd seen in the tutorial. I knew I could now resign without leaving anything undone for the company or me. I did so.

I was soon back to feeling periods of frustration … I still hadn't found my dream job. I turned next to video production, as I had a sudden fascination with the industry. I applied myself to the task of producing a documentary about the pros and cons of vaccines. Several months later, I realized it was too controversial for mainstream television. Fortuitously, my daughter and son-in-law were in the process of building a newly founded company to manufacture electromagnetic units for health. They started with a demand from family and friends. With the endorsement of the scientist who was lecturing about the technology and word-of-mouth, their sales soon soared.

As caretakers to bring this technology to the world, they wanted to provide as much information as possible about both the technology and natural health to those who were open and interested. That's where my skills fit. I was invited to join the company. At the age of 58, I found my niche!

Now as I am researching, writing, and assisting with video productions about natural ways to better health, I get great satisfaction from hearing how people from all over the world are being helped with their health. By listening and acting on my inner nudges, I've learned to trust Spirit. I've also learned that Spirit helps to manifest our goals in a greater and better way than we can possibly dream.

~ *Carole Punt*

About the Author

(Darlene Montgomery is a writer, editor, and respected authority on dreams who speaks to groups and organizations on uplifting subjects. Her first book, *Dream Yourself Awake,* chronicled the journey she took to discover her own divine mission using dreams, waking dreams, and intuition.

As a consultant she has also helped compile two of the famous Chicken Soup books. Her stories have appeared in *Chicken Soup for the Parent's Soul* and *Chicken Soup for the Canadian Soul.* In addition, they have also been featured on The WTN website and published in *Vitality Magazine* and *Synchronicity Magazine.* Darlene's recent book media campaign took her across Canada and the U.S., where she appeared on national television and radio shows, including Michael Coren Live, Rogers Daytime, ON TV News, Breakfast Television, The Patty Purcell Show, The Life Station, and more. Darlene also operates her own public relations firm, helping to promote authors and experts.

For more on Darlene and her work visit www.lifedreams.org.

Other Books by *Darlene Montgomery*

Dream Yourself Awake

This autobiography reads like a spiritual mystery. A question asked by a mysterious guide sets the author on a journey to uncover the source of her deep spiritual illness, leading her to discover the one deep truth that needs to be understood for her to be healed. Throughout the story, hundreds of personal dreams act as clues to solve the mystery and lead to a personal revelation for the author.

Dreams are a natural homing device residing in the heart of soul. Many of us are aware of a yearning or sense of destiny, purpose, or mission we must find before our life is complete. In *Dream Yourself Awake*, Darlene Montgomery tells the story behind the search for her own mission in a series of dreams, waking dreams, and inner experiences. As we share her journey, we will discover how to use these same tools to see beyond the illusions of the mind and travel straight into the heart of our divine purpose.

ISBN: 0-9683402-0-2 • 175 pages • PB

First in the Series,

Conscious Women—
Conscious Lives:

Powerful & Transformational
Stories of Healing Body Mind
& Soul

Edited by Darlene Montgomery

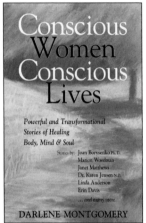

In this extraordinary collection of personal revelation, women share their deepest and heart-felt experiences of healing from loss, illness and accident. These stories show how the journey of facing some of life's greatest obstacles can be followed by a joyous emergence from the darkness of despair, and a return to the light of life, love and new wisdom.

These true stories by women, for women, help open the heart, heal the spirit, and bring peace of mind during some of life's most challenging times. As each author brings a treasure from her own rich experience, she contributes to the pool of wisdom we share on this planet of how each of us can meet our greatest fears to rise again with wisdom, grace and courage.

Whatever challenges you presently face, these stories offer hope, reassurance, comfort and proud examples of the resilient nature and wisdom of women.

ISBN 0-9734186-1-3 • 216 pages • PB • Cdn $19.95 US $13.95

Second in the Series,

Conscious Women—
Conscious Lives:

**Women Share More Life-
Transforming Stories of Healing,
Triumphing Over Death and
Scaling the Heights to Achieve
Their Greatest Dreams**

Edited by Darlene Montgomery

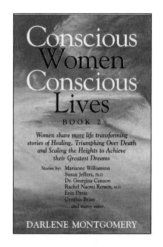

This second collection of stories brings together women from across North America, writing about rising out of extraordinary circumstances, facing fear and adversity head on, and healing through love. These stories will inspire and motivate women to find the love that is both within themselves and around them, to meet the challenges life gives them.

> *"[These] stories will lead you gently through
> the barrier of fear to the pathway of hope.
> What a wonderful book!"*
> — *Colleen Smith, author,* The Pocket Guide to Your Heart

ISBN 0-973670-50-9 • 200 pages • PB • Cdn $19.95 US $13.95

Contributors

SYBIL BARBOUR resides in Kitchener, Ontario with her husband and an aged cat. She is a retired registered nurse and midwife. She recently fulfilled a lifelong dream of traveling to Italy, Greece, Scotland, and New Zealand. You can contact her at *sybilbarbour@ sympatico.ca.*

NELL BERRY is a newly published author of *Growing Up In Missouri and Other Short Stories,* which may be purchased from www.publishamerica.com, Amazon.com or Barnes & Noble. She is 74 years old and has four children, nine grandchildren, and two great granddaughters. Her husband of 55 years is a woodworker who can build just about anything out of wood. Nell's activities include sewing, crocheting, cooking, and, of course, writing poems, song lyrics and short stories. She is a regular attendee at her church and loves to sing the gospel songs.

CYNTHIA BRIAN, *New York Times* best-selling co-author of *Chicken Soup for the Gardener's Soul,* author of *Be the Star You Are!®, 99 Gifts for Living, Loving, Laughing, and Learning to Make a Difference, The Business of Show Business,* and *Miracle Moments®,* is an internationally acclaimed keynote speaker, personal growth consultant, host of radio and TV shows, syndicated columnist, and acting coach. Often referred to by the media as "the Renaissance woman with soul!" Cynthia is a world traveler who speaks French, Spanish, Italian, and Dutch. With nearly three decades of experience working in the entertainment field as an actor, producer, writer, coach, designer, and casting director, she has had the honor of performing with some of the biggest names in the industry. She is the Founder/CEO of the 501(c)(3) charity, Be the Star You Are! that empowers families and youth at risk through literacy and positive media. Her motto is "To be a leader, you must be a reader!" Cynthia is dedicated to helping others achieve their dreams by implementing their unique gifts, and she has coached many aspiring thespians, writers, and professionals to fame and fortune. For more information contact Cynthia Brian at Starstyle® Productions, LLC, PO Box 422, Moraga, CA 94556 925-377-STAR (7827). www.star-style.com, www.starstyleproductions.com www.bethestaryouare.org

JULIA CAMERON is an active artist who teaches internationally. A poet, playwright, fiction writer, and essayist, she has extensive credits in film, television, and theater, and she is an award-winning journalist. She is author of the best-selling book on creative practice, *The Artist's Way*, and has taught and refined her methods for nearly two decades.

GEORGINA CANNON is a Board Certified Hypnotherapist, a Doctor of Metaphysical Counseling, NLP Master, Timeline practitioner, and Past Life Regression Therapist. In addition, she is an accredited instructor for the National Guild of Hypnotists, the Medical and Dental Hypnotherapy Association, and the International Board of Regression Therapies. She is recognized by many in the media as "The Source" for expert opinion in the field of hypnotherapy and issues around complementary wellness treatments, and she regularly meets with medical and wellness professionals to enhance their knowledge and awareness of hypnosis, past life journeys, and the dynamic healing potential of soul.

She is also on the Advisory Board of the National Guild of Hypnotists. She facilitates past life research and regression sessions, and specializes in enabling clients to achieve major life changes, healing personal and emotional issues. Dr. Cannon has been featured in many national print and broadcast news articles and television programs, including a three-part, one-hour series on CBC Television, broadcast in the fall of 2004. She is a regular guest on the Shirley MacLaine on-line radio show, where she offers advice on past life regression and related topics. Her book *Return: Experience the Power of the Past, Past Life Regression and You* takes the reader on a personal journey of exploration through past life research and regression. For more on Georgina Cannon, visit www.ont-hypnosis-centre.com or call 416-489-0333 (out of town calls: 1-866-497-7469).

DARLENE CHRISTIANSON currently lives north of Toronto with her wonderful husband Tom and son Brandon, of whom she is extremely proud of. She is also inspired by the work ethics of her lovely daughter Farris-lee who is entering her second year of university. They are her pride and joy. She wears a "few hats" these days within her career. Darlene designs and sells homes for a Canadian manufacturer. She also co-hosts a local entertainment and lifestyle show called "Daytime" on Rogers Television as well as assisting her husband with his company Venture Bound Tours. She lives her life always looking for new adventures ahead of her. Her email is *gbay@rogers.com*, and her website is www.ventureboundtours

SUZANNE K. COY, of African and Indigenous descent, graduated from the National Theatre School and has taught Transformational Acting Workshops across North America. Suzanne, or Zan for short, is a multi-talented artist, poet, producer, and storyteller. Zan has numerous credits as an actor in film, television, and theatre. She has tailor-made various corporate workshops, including 'Creating a Stress-Free Workplace.' Her mission is to train people to be certified laughers who go on to laugh all the time for no reason. After 20 years she continues to lend her talents toward developing and facilitating children's workshops that use creativity to teach life skills. Zan wrote, directed, and produced the successful one-woman show, 'Avoid the Void,' which played in Anaheim, California, and Edmonton,

Alberta. As founder of Lovetown Productions, she has written and performed many comedic sketches, poems, and cultural stories for the various communities. She studied Consulting for Communities of Color in Oakland, California, and she is an associate member of the National Community Development Institute. She feels the role of the artist is to activate transformation in oneself and the community.

She is currently touring her new comedic one woman show as well as producing a multicultural television show that merges the genres of situation comedy, stand-up and sketch comedy. With writers Neil Ross and Sharon Temple, as well as Historic Site Coordinator Cara Reeves, she is presenting "The Peace Rights and Freedoms Game: A Canadian History for the Classroom." This story chronicles events from the First Nations and the Children of Peace, whose ideas led to Responsible Government and to the Canadian Charter of Rights. This participatory experiential approach to the history of democracy in Canada uses theatre games, mask, dance, drum, stand-up comedy, and rap to engage students in the democratic process, prepare them to be critical voters, explore character and key values in the development of Canadian society, and apply these values to their own lives and modern situations. Suzanne can be reached at *hu_more@yahoo.com*.

CAROLYN DEMARCO is a physician and author. She was one of the first to advocate the proactive approach to health. Throughout her career, she has advocated on behalf of women's rights to make informed choices about drugs and surgery. She was a pioneer in natural childbirth and a leading proponent of midwifery. She counsels women and men to use safe natural alternatives whenever possible. She has written two books, *Take Charge of Your Body, Women's Health Advisor* and *Dr. DeMarco Answers Your Questions*. Her work can be viewed at www.demarcomd.com. She is currently working on a third book entitled *Overcoming Life's Tsunamis*.

LORI DAVILA is a nationally recognized career/life coach, recruiting expert, and author. She specializes in strategically shaping career changers' unique competitive advantages and making connections that attract exciting job leads. For corporations, Lori directs large-scale hiring initiatives. She writes a career and networking column for *The Atlanta Journal-Constitution* and regularly contributes to *The Wall Street Journal*. Lori's book, *How to Choose the Right Person for the Right Job Every Time* (McGraw-Hill), includes 401 behavior-based and other interview questions for both hiring managers and job seekers. Lori has appeared on numerous radio programs and in national publications.

DONNA EDEN is one of the world's most effective healers. Able from childhood to clairvoyantly see the body's subtle energies, she not only works with those energies to further health, happiness, and vitality, she has made a career of teaching people who do not see subtle energies how to work with them—joyfully and effectively. She has treated over 10,000 individual clients and has taught hundreds of classes, speaking to packed houses throughout the United States, Europe, Australia, New Zealand and South America.

Donna consistently exhilarates and amazes her audiences. She offers exciting, empowering, invaluable classes that can be attended by laypeople as well as professionals. More and more of her work is becoming available in books and video training programs.

When **LAILA GHATTAS** isn't gallivanting around the world facilitating life-altering retreats, she offers Truly Madly Deeply workshops in Toronto to individuals and corporations. Laila is an artist, Gestalt therapist, Reiki practitioner, sea kayaker and founder of Aziza Healing Adventures. She designs and leads workshops and retreats for women, men, couples, youths and mixed groups who seek true personal growth. Her passionate belief in the combined healing power of creativity, nature, psychotherapy and movement manifests in wellness programs that deliver creative self-discovery and gentle eco-journeys in Canada, Mexico, Bali, Europe and the South Pacific.

Laila speaks and publishes on creativity, the power of language, self-acceptance and compassion, and the healing benefits of retreats. She has a private therapy practice in Toronto. Her paintings are reproduced on Delicious Wearables, a line of colorful aprons, tote bags, prints and other unique gifts.

Laila holds a Bachelor of Fine Arts in Visual Art, Bachelor of Education, Ontario Teachers Certificate, Certificate in Gestalt Therapy, Certificate in Expressive Art, and Usui Reiki degrees I and II. Look for her book, *Impeccable Leadership: Compassion at Work*, a must-have handbook for progressive corporations. Contact Laila at *laila@aziza.ca* or visit her on line at www.aziza.ca

KAREN HAFFEY is from and currently living in Toronto, Canada. She has also studied, worked and played in Montreal, Vancouver, and Santa Fe, New Mexico. She runs her own creative wellness company called *kultivate*, reaching out to individuals and groups to facilitate self-growth and community, and works with people in long-term care offering complementary therapies and creative programming.

Karen earned a Bachelor of Fine Arts from Concordia University, certification in Polarity Therapy and Cranial Sacral Therapy from the New Mexico Academy of Healing Arts, and has other training and experience with the private and nonprofit sectors and in the field of complementary healthcare. She is an avid and published writer and, in general, a seeker of ways to live from her creative soul! It is her intention to experience, inspire, and encourage creative healing that cultivates body, mind, and spirit. For more information, please visit www.kultivate.ca or contact Karen directly by e-mailing *karen@kultivate.ca.*

ELLIE BRAUN-HALEY lives in an old country home where she can walk the countryside and feel the nearness of God. She says, "There will be more stories because I believe the contacts will continue, even increase. The tie to my son remains, and I hold onto the words he gave me in a dream: 'But, Mom, death is not forever.'" Her book,

A Little Door, A Little Light, ISBN 1-894446-92-X, is available through Eagle Valley Research (evrcanada.com). Look on the Menu bar for Eagle Creek Publishers at the web address) or contact Ellie at *shaley@telusplanet.net.*

SUSAN HIGGINS grew up on the high plains of Wyoming, and life has taken her far from her Western roots. Marriage and raising a family took precedence over her girl-reporter dreams, yet the love of the written word has never been far from her heart. These days Susan uses her life experiences and spiritual insights to write short stories, articles, and poems from her home in central Pennsylvania. When she isn't writing, Susan can be found running her own fudge and ice cream business in Lancaster's Historic Central Market. You can visit her website at www.PennsylvaniaFudgeCompany.com.

MONIQUE HOWAT is a youth motivator and the founder of Confident Girls and Guys. She presents self-esteem and character-building workshops at elementary and high schools in and around the Toronto area. Monique offers training on the principles of self-esteem, public speaking, coaching for parents or teens, leadership for women and consultation services for at-risk youth programming. You can visit her website at www.confidentgirlsguys.com

MAXINE HYNDMAN is the author of the recently published book *The Naked Millionaire*. As a money and marketing coach, Maxine has helped hundreds of individuals make financial leaps in their lives by sharing her unique perspective on the relationship between ourselves and our money and the inevitable, dynamic connection between 'whealth'—a healthy relationship with money—and marketing that we eventually come to in our journey to abundance. As a money and marketing coach, she focuses specifically on how to allow whealth through the power of authentic self-promotion.

Maxine can be contacted by email at *maxine@thenakedmillionaire.com.* Find out more about 'whealth' at the website: www.thenakedmillionaire.com.

KAREN JEFFERY spent a lifetime as an entrepreneur, establishing and managing many businesses on the US mainland, in Hawaii, and throughout the South Pacific islands. A passionate, experienced businesswoman, for 35 years she directed her various companies: dance studios, an arts company, a macadamia farm, a restaurant and catering business, an international brokerage, investment and management firms, and several non-profits and islander causes. Finally Karen took a one-year sabbatical. Three years later, she has rediscovered her life-long passion for writing and resurrected a body of work reaching back further than her professional career. Following her bliss, she now writes novels, short stories, and poems from her hilltop home in beautiful Maui.

SUSAN JEFFERS, PH.D. Few people have helped change as many lives as much-loved author and leading self-help authority Susan Jeffers, Ph.D., who first captured the world's heart nearly twenty years ago with her acclaimed book *Feel the Fear and Do It Anyway*. Sales of Susan's numerous best-selling works are in the millions, reaching more than 100 countries and translated into over 36 languages.

Susan is best known for her teachings on overcoming fear, healing relationships, and moving forward in life with confidence, joy and love. Susan's eighteen titles to date also include *Feel the Fear and Beyond*, *End the Struggle and Dance with Life*, *Embracing Uncertainty*, *The Little Book of Confidence*, *The Little Book of Peace of Mind*, *I Can Handle It!* (a manual for young children), *Life is Huge!* and *The Feel the Fear Guide to Lasting Love*. Susan has also authored the Fear-Less series of affirmation books and audios.

In 2004, the *Times* of the U.K. named Susan "the Queen of Self-Help," ranking her alongside such influential gurus as Nelson Mandela, the Dalai Lama, and Deepak Chopra. A year earlier, the popular spiritual consciousness magazine *Kindred Spirit* gave Susan the award for Best Personal Development Book of the year. As well as being a celebrated workshop leader and speaker, Susan has appeared on Oprah numerous times and many other national and international radio and television shows.

Susan's popular website, www.susanjeffers.com, is widely visited for her daily affirmation, Feel the Fear stories, and her monthly article. She recently launched a new company, Jeffers Press, in order to publish her own books and those of other inspirational writers. Susan received her master's degree and doctorate in psychology from Columbia University. She lives in Los Angeles, California with her husband, Mark Shelmerdine.

SYLVIA JONG has been a student of Eckankar for the past 25 years. She flies for a major Canadian carrier and is a member of its emergency response team. A former hospice volunteer, she now devotes her free time to working with a special child who does not speak and has other complex challenges.

SUE KENNEY Pilgrim. Author. Speaker. Leader. Following a successful international career in the high tech industry, Sue was suddenly downsized, so she decided to go for a long hike on the Camino de Santiago de Compostela; a medieval pilgrimage route in Spain. She walked 780 kilometers, alone in the winter. When she returned home, she developed an artistic practice focused on inspirational speaking, writing, and delivering workshops based on a philosophy of principled leadership. Sue wrote, produced, and recorded a storytelling CD called *Stone by Stone*. Her first book, *My Camino*, has attracted international fame, and is well on its way to becoming a national best seller. By applying the discipline learned as a master's world class rower, she endeavors to tell her stories through a variety of mediums which also includes publishing a monthly newsletter, documentary filmmaking, co-writing a screenplay based on her book, and storytelling. After spending over 20 years in corporate business, Sue now balances a creative artistic approach with the business of being an entrepreneur aligned with her life purpose to inspire others. Sue now lives at her lakeside home north of

Toronto. Sue has been seen on Breakfast Television Toronto/Halifax, Good Morning Canada, Omni's Fineprint, Rogers, CTV, CBC Radio and more. *My Camino* is available at bookstores. Sue's website is www.suekenney.ca

JO LEONARD has presented talks and workshops for over 20 years throughout the United States and in Mexico, Canada, Australia, New Zealand, Europe, and West Africa. Her first two novel-length works of fiction are currently making the rounds of publishers, as are numerous short stories. In addition to speaking and writing, she serves as the Vice President of a commercial printing company. Jo lives in Occoquan, Virginia, a historic village 15 miles south of Washington D.C., with much-loved husband Jerry and two Siamese cats. She may be contacted at *jlionhart@aol.com*.

CÉSAN D'ORNELLAS LEVINE is a visual artist. Her work ranges from expressive symbolism to purely abstract. The themes of her color- and texture-rich art orbit around symbols and iconography from diverse religious and mythological streams. The paintings are a search for a universal mystical truth—the common denominator of meaning shared by all. César's work, both inner and outer, represents a deep commitment towards the spiritual.

César has home and studio in Richmond Hill, Ontario, Canada with her husband and two daughters. Her fine art work can be viewed at www.cesan.ca and she can be contacted at *cesan@cesan.ca*

JAYE LEWIS is a devout Christian and an award winning writer who looks at life from a unique perspective, celebrating the miraculous in the every day. Jaye lives with her family in the Appalachian Mountains of Virginia, USA. Jaye is a prolific freelance writer and contributing author to the *Chicken Soup for the Soul* series. Read more of Jaye's stories at her website www.entertainingangels.org or email her at *jayelewis@comcast.net*.

DEBORAH MALTMAN is a Life-Centered Transformational Psychotherapist and Intuitive Catalyst for Healing currently residing in Guelph, Ontario, Canada. Deborah is interested in traditional healing and energy healing. She is a student of *A Course in Miracles*, and her work is guided by her soul's passions, which include offering her skills as a therapist and marketing fair-trade items from the Kalahari Bushmen of Africa. Deborah is an expert in working with autism. She has a nomadic spirit, believes in miracles, and teaches self-healing. Deborah can be reached by email at *realizinghealth @hotmail.com* or *dmaltman@execulink.com*.

JACQUELYN MANTELL has always maintained an avid interest in healing ever since being wrongly diagnosed as an epileptic when she was a teenager. She has traveled the world over with her doctor husband to attend medical seminars about holistic medicine and new methods of treatment. They work side by side in their medical clinic where Jacquelyn, among other duties, facilitates patient healing by doing holistic counseling with patients. This includes nutritional education along with emotional, mental and spiritual guidance. As co-hosts of a medical talk show, she and her husband have discussed all aspects of holistic healing. Jacquelyn loves to write and teach others about spiritual awareness and how to recognize God's love in their daily lives. She has been a member of the Eckankar clergy for many years. Contact Jackie at *bluestar9@adelphia.net*.

TERESA MILLER was born and educated in Europe. She works in the fashion business and loves painting and walking. She is the mother of two children. Her life goal is to become a better person, learning how to love others at all times.

KAREN THOMAS PETHERICK discovered her passion for books in 1993. Little did she know that working in the printing industry, she was being groomed for her future career.

Many people don't experience the opportunity of making a

career out of their passion, but she has. A book designer with over 300 books carrying her name, she began her journey with the first book *A Country Outhouse* by John H. Passmore. Shortly afterward, her second project was to redesign Robin S. Sharma's book *MegaLiving.* She worked again with Robin on *A Monk Who Sold His Ferrari* designing the interior layout and coordinating the printing of the book.

Karen works closely with her clients, guiding them through the publishing experience. From evaluation, editing, design, and co-ordination of printing and distribution, she achieves professional, high quality publications.

Over the years clients have included Dr. Georgina Cannon, Sue Kenney, Robin S. Sharma, Julie E. Czerneda, Colleen Hoffman-Smith, White Knight Publications, Fitzhenry & Whiteside, Chapters/Indigo, and Darlene Montgomery. Books of inspiration, humor, poetry, history and self-help are just a few of the genres that she has designed.

Karen lived and raised her three children in the greater Toronto area. In 2001 she moved to the country where she now owns a home on a quiet country acre lot. She is quite proud to be a part of the team of the successful *Conscious Women* series. She can be reached at *kpetherick@rogers.com* or call 613-482-4427.

JUDY PRANG resides in Kingston, Ontario with her husband, Cal. She is a Senior Manager for a major financial institution and volun-teers her time on the Board of Directors of The Elizabeth Fry Society of Kingston, an organization that supports women in conflict, or in danger of coming into conflict with the law. As she developed her communication, facilitation and motivational skills, Judy learned that storytelling is a holy way to celebrate our spiritual journeys. Mother of two grown daughters and grandmother of five, she is currently exploring ways to help others record their own family stories as well as working on her first book. Judy can be reached at *judyprang@hotmail.com.*

JANE PIPER is founder and director of SAAV: Survivors & Artists for Abolishing Violence. She is also an actor, writer, political activist, events producer, and rape survivor. Jane grew up in London, Ontario, Canada, and did her BFA in Theatre at Concordia University in Montreal. She has been living in California for more than 10 years. In San Francisco, Jane produced many events from concerts to raves, inspiring her to get involved with social and political activism. Having founded the Next School Collective, she organized several First Amendment rallies. In 1998 she produced "Progress: the Emerging Culture", a cross-cultural arts and communications event showcasing the potential of electronic dance culture. Jane was also the Children's Program Coordinator for the San Francisco Whole Life Expo, where she and her collective created the Next School Children's Creativity Centre. She has been a featured guest speaker at many events, including the Whole Life Expo, where she spoke alongside many influential people, her most memorable being author Ken Kesey.

Leaving the Bay Area behind to pursue her acting career, Jane moved to LA and attended the American Academy of Dramatic Arts. She has appeared in HBO's Curb Your Enthusiasm and a few independent films. Since her brutal attack in 2003, Jane has once again become active as a public speaker. She is now sharing her story, with the intention of spreading awareness on the issue of rape and the healing process that follows. Jane has had the opportunity to speak alongside some fantastic artists also focused on ending violence: Jane Fonda, Eve Ensler (creator of *The Vagina Monologues* and *The Good Body*), and actors Jennifer Garner and David Schwimmer. She is a contributing author in *Raising Humanity: Birthing Our Global Family* by Rhobbin Alexis, for which 10% of the book proceeds go to **SAAV**. Currently, Jane is living in Marina Del Rey and creating a one-woman show exploring the experience of her assault and how violence has affected her life and the world around her. If you would like to find out more about **SAAV** or make a contribution, please go to www.ContactSAAV.org or write to Jane at *info@ContactSAAV.org*.

JANE DURST-PULKYS is a nutritionist with degrees in both the clinical and holistic arenas. While managing a busy practice in Toronto, she has appeared on television broadcasts, facilitated workshops or talks around the world, and done nutritional counseling for a number of F500 companies. She can be contacted at *jane@live-bloodcell.ca*.

CAROLE PUNT and her husband enjoy their home in Penticton, British Columbia in concert with, and under the auspices of two cats. Mugs and Tigger reluctantly allow granddogs visiting rights. Two of her most recently published works are a story that appeared in *Angel Cats: Divine Messengers of Co*mfort by Allen and Linda Anderson and a booklet, *Electricity for Health in the 21st Century*. She has enjoyed interviews on radio and television and acted in community theatre. As a member of the clergy, she gives talks and facilitates workshops. A hike along the lake always beckons. *carole@punt.ca*

BETTY JANE RAPIN, nicknamed BJ, is a clergywoman who is currently the Eckankar Spiritual Services Director for the state of Pennsylvania. She is a writer whose works have been published in a book of poetry and in magazines, newspapers, and newsletters. Some of her stories can be found on websites at www.eckankrofpa.org and www.eckankar-WV.org. These stories are also being translated into Spanish.

Betty has appeared on television and radio shows where she was interviewed about a variety of spiritual subjects. Now retired, she continues to freelance her writing. She is presently working on her first book while teaching adult education at Penn Trafford High School. As well Betty is a public speaker and a lover of life. The motto that appears on her business card reads, *"Love puts a smile in your heart, and on your face."*

LAURA REAVE, PH. D. has been a writer, editor, and English professor for fifteen years. Her current research interest is spiritual leadership, and she had an article on this topic published in 2005 in the journal *Leadership Quarterly*. She has a particular interest in spiritual poetry. She is proud to have served as the text editor for *Conscious Women, Conscious Lives Book Two* as well as *Conscious Women, Conscious Careers*. She can be reached at *lreave@ody.ca*.

JANINE GWENDOLINE SMITH is a Renaissance artist whose love for life fuels her passionate creativity. Defying definition and category, Janine reaches out to share rare sensitivity and vision as Spirit moves her. She pursues excellence in her disciplines of singing, songwriting, painting, design, clay sculpture, poetry, acting and T'ai Chi. In 2002, Janine released her first solo CD, "LOVE LIVES INSIDE," and has one BRAVO! Video from that CD to date. Janine's music is eclectic, international, and universal, with exquisite arrangements. Her vocal style has been compared to the likes of Sarah Brightman, Kate Bush, Ella Fitzgerald and Elaine Paige. When asked what kind of music she performs, Janine responds, "Beautiful Music." Janine also loves Jazz Standards and can torch a song with her fluidic range.

Janine has always had a great love for visual art and has expressed herself eclectically in this media all her life. At one of her exhibits, an art critic said, "So this is a group show, right?" Love of nature, exaltation of Woman, exploration of our place in the cosmos, attention to detail, delight in color, and strong Asian influence (from three decades of T'ai Chi practice) are all evident in her art. Janine's path is an infinite quest; her purpose is to unfold greater and greater expression of the Divine Potential within.

DR. SHERYL VALENTINE is a chiropractor who has been practicing in Southern California since 1985. She has lectured on spiritual principles since 1993, and she has a new book based on her lectures due in Spring 2006, entitled, *Oh My God, It's ME! www.sheryl-valentine.com*

JACKIE WOODS is the founder of the Adawehi Institute Healing School and Wellness Center in Columbus, N.C. She lives there in a community that holds the intent of empowering the heart for extraordinary living. She has authored several books and numerous CDs. These teachings, along with her internet classes, are now available from the jackiewoods.org web site.

Permissions / Notes

Don't Let Rejection Stop You!, by Susan Jeffers, Ph.D. reprinted from *Life is Huge!* published by Jeffers Press, pages 20 to 23, Copyright © 2000 and 2004.

How Césan Got Her Groove Back, reprinted by permission of Césan d'Ornellas Levine © 2005 Césan d'Ornellas Levine

A Road Less Traveled, reprinted by permission of Maxine Hyndman © 2005 Maxine Hyndman

Spreading My Wings, reprinted by permission of Georgina Cannon © 2005 Georgina Cannon

It's Personal, reprinted by permission of Jaye Lewis © 2005 Jaye Lewis

Becoming Who I Really Am, reprinted by permission of Judy Conlin Prang © 2005 Judy Conlin Prang

A Gift of Love, reprinted by permission of Sybil Barbour © 2005 Sybil Barbour

A Soul Calling, reprinted by permission of Karen Jeffery © 2005 Karen Jeffery

Before You, reprinted by permission of Laura Reave© 2005 Laura Reave

Winter Fog, reprinted by permission of Laura Reave © 2005 Laura Reave

It Started with a Dream, reprinted by permission of Carole Punt © 2005 Carole Punt

Where the Truth Lies, reprinted by permission of Suzanne Coy © 2005 Suzanne Coy

Time is a Gift, reprinted by permission of Karen Thomas Petherick © 2005 Karen Thomas Petherick

Employed by Love, reprinted by permission of Laila Ghattas © 2005 Laila Ghattas

My Invisible Hands, reprinted by permission of Lori Davila © 2005 Lori Davila

My Journey, reprinted by permission of Darlene Christianson © 2005 Darlene Christianson

Perfect Casting, reprinted by permission of Janine Gwendoline Smith © 2005 Janine Gwendoline Smith

Healing My Heart, reprinted by permission of Jaye Lewis © 2005 Jaye Lewis

From an Ocean of Tears, reprinted by permission of Carolyn Demarco © 2005 Carolyn Demarco

Reaching Into Myself, reprinted by permission of Karen Haffey © 2005 Karen Haffey

Connecting to a Higher Purpose, reprinted by permission of Jane Piper © 2005 Jane Piper

A Matter of Perspective, reprinted by permission of Janine Gwendoline Smith © 2005 Janine Gwendoline Smith

Notes

1   Jacob A. Riss—Writer, Social Activist 1901

OTHER WHITE KNIGHT BOOKS

Adoption	A Swim Against The Tide, *David R.I. McKinstry*
Biography	The Life and Times of Nancy Ford-Inman, *Nancy Erb Kee*
Education	From Student to Citizen, *Prof. Peter Hennessy*
Health	Prescription for Patience, *Dr. Kevin J Leonard* Brain Injury, *Alan J. Cooper*
Humour	By ***David R.I. McKinstry***: • An Innkeeper's Discretion BOOK ONE • An Innkeeper's Discretion BOOK TWO Will That Be Cash or 'Cuffs?, *Yvonne Blackwood*
Inspiration	"Oh My God. It's ME!", *Dr. Sheryl Valentine* By ***Rev. Dr. John S. Niles***: • The Art of Sacred Parenting • How I Became Father to 1000 Children By ***Darlene Montgomery***: • Conscious Women, Conscious Lives ONE • Conscious Women, Conscious Lives TWO • Conscious Women, Conscious Careers Happiness: Use It or Lose It, *Rev. Dr. David "Doc" Loomis* Sharing MS (Multiple Sclerosis), *Linda Ironside* Sue Kenney's My Camino, *Sue Kenney*
Personal Finances	Don't Borrow $Money$, *Paul E Counter*
Poetry	Loveplay, *Joe Fromstein and Linda Stitt* Two Voices, A Circle of Love, *Serena Williamson Andrew*
Politics & History	Prophets of Violence, Prophets of Peace, *Dr. K. Sohail* Turning Points, *Ray Argyle*
Self-Help	By ***Dr. K. Sohail*** • The Art of Living in Your Green Zone • The Art of Loving in Your Green Zone, • The Art of Working in Your Green Zone, *with Bette Davis* • Love, Sex and Marriage, *with Bette Davis*
True Crime – Police	"10-45" Spells Death, *Kathy McCormack Carter* Life on Homicide, *Former Police Chief Bill McCormack* The Myth of The Chosen One, *Dr. K. Sohail*

Visit our website www.whiteknightbooks.ca or request catalogue.

RECOMMENDED READING FROM OTHER PUBLISHERS

History	An Amicable Friendship (Canadiana), *Jan Th. J. Krijff*
Religion	From Islam to Secular Humanism, *Dr. K. Sohail*
Biography	Gabriel's Dragon, *Arch Priest Fr. Antony Gabriel*
Epic Poetry	Pro Deo, *Prof. Ronald Morton Smith*